MUCHINGA SIMBULE

God's Prescription for Wealth Creation

First edition

This book was professionally typeset on Reedsy.
Find out more at reedsy.com

To my beloved wife and children—

Your unwavering support has been the quiet strength behind every word in these pages. You have given me the space to reflect, to meditate, and to shape my thoughts into what is now this book.

For your patience, your love, and your understanding, I am forever grateful.

This work is as much yours as it is mine.

Dear Reader,

While money can provide a sense of security, true 'wealth' encompasses much more. It includes physical and mental well-being, fulfilling relationships, and deep personal connections.

This book offers a profound opportunity to embrace God's blueprint for creating lasting wealth and abundance.

So, find a comfortable spot, open your heart, and enjoy each page. May this be the beginning of your journey toward true, God-centered wealth.

Uplifting and thought-provoking, this book does not just inform- it inspires. Highly recommended for those in pursuit of personal growth and spiritual fulfilment.

— Mrs Renee Chikwanda
Author, Educator, and Social Advisor

God's Prescription for Wealth Creation is an absolute classic for anyone seeking to engage their minds in intellectual discourse and philosophical perspectives.

This book masterfully combines timeless biblical wisdom with insights from renowned thinkers, past and present, to argue that wealth is your birthright.

The conclusion is clear: our active cooperation with God sets us on the path to success in every area of life. This book challenges us to rise above our limitations, expand our horizons, and harness the boundless potential of our minds.

By embracing the principles and wisdom from God's word, we can unleash our greatness, make a profound impact on society, and ultimately fulfill our wealthy destiny as God intended. I enthusiastically recommend this book.

— Happy Mulwe
Author, Meet You At The Top

Contents

Foreword

There are books that enlighten the mind, and then there are books that awaken the heart. God's Prescription for Wealth Creation does both. It offers a profound revelation of what truly resonates with the divine.

At its core, this book unveils a powerful truth: genuine wealth isn't merely about accumulation, but about the profound act of service. True prosperity, the author argues, is not measured by the figures in your bank account, but by the tangible, positive impact you create in the lives of others. It challenges conventional notions, asserting that in God's eyes, service far surpasses mere sacrifice. The offerings we bring to the altar of life only gain true meaning when they flow from a heart that genuinely seeks to honor and uplift those around us.

This book lays bare a profound reality that work is not given to us solely to fill our bank accounts, but to enrich lives—instilling hope, restoring dignity, and spreading light. It is in this act of serving that true and lasting prosperity is discovered. This isn't just a biblical principle; it's a universal truth, beautifully echoed in the fulfilling lives of those who embrace a purpose beyond themselves.

For anyone seeking a deeper, more meaningful perspective on wealth and the very essence of life, God's Prescription for Wealth Creation provides the perfect, powerful dose. Regardless of your current circumstances—whether you're experiencing abundance or searching for deeper purpose—this book will challenge your assumptions, ignite your spirit, and fundamentally reshape your understanding of what success truly entails.

This is a book you will proudly cherish, not just because you've read it, but because its wisdom will fundamentally alter the way you live, knowing that it has opened your mind and heart to what genuinely matters most in life.

Dr. Kachinga Agrippa Sichizya
Founder and CEO, By His Stripes (BHS) Specialist Medical Center
Lusaka, Zambia
Award winning author, Uneasy Yoke

Introduction

Every person, regardless of background or circumstance, shares a deep desire for a life filled with happiness, security, and purpose. We all long for well-being—not just in terms of material wealth, but also in relationships, health, and personal fulfillment. Yet, despite this shared aspiration, many people struggle to find true prosperity. Why? Because the road to a flourishing life is often clouded by misleading beliefs, societal expectations, and unclear definitions of what success really means.

This book serves as a guide to uncovering the timeless, divine principles that lead to genuine wealth and fulfillment. Rather than promoting get-rich-quick schemes, we will explore how work—when understood and approached correctly—becomes a sacred tool for creating abundance. According to this divine design, prosperity is not just about accumulating money; it is about aligning our efforts with a higher purpose, contributing value to the world, and experiencing the deep satisfaction that comes from meaningful labor.

To build a clear and practical understanding, we will carefully define essential concepts such as wealth, work, etc. By examining how these ideas connect, we will reveal the core principles that lead to a life of significance—one where financial stability, personal growth, and positive impact go hand in hand.

Whether you are seeking financial freedom, a deeper sense of calling, or simply a more balanced and joyful existence, this book will provide the insights needed to navigate the journey with wisdom and confidence.

The path to prosperity is not a mystery reserved for a lucky few; it is a divine blueprint available to all who are willing to learn, apply, and trust in the process.

Definition of Key Terms and Concepts

Work

Work, as a concept, extends far beyond the mere execution of tasks for remuneration. It represents a purposeful engagement with the world, a deliberate act of contributing to the collective well-being of society. In its essence, work is the manifestation of human potential, the translation of innate abilities into tangible value.

> Anthony Giddens, in his groundbreaking work "Sociology," defines work as ***"the carrying out of tasks requiring the expenditure of mental and physical effort, which has as its objective the production of goods and services that cater to human needs."***

This definition highlights the dual nature of work, encompassing both the physical exertion and the intellectual engagement necessary to create value.

However, work is not merely a means to an end; it is an essential part of the human experience, a fundamental expression of our purpose and potential. It is through work that we cultivate our skills, develop our character, and contribute to the advancement of society. Work transforms raw materials into finished products, innovative ideas into practical solutions, and human potential into societal progress.

In the context of this book, work is viewed as a sacred calling, a divine mandate to steward the resources entrusted to us and to contribute to the flourishing of humanity. It is an act of co-creation with God, a partnership in the ongoing work of building a better world.

Prescription

The term **"prescription"** carries a diverse meaning, encompassing both directive authority and remedial guidance. According to the New Webster Dictionary of the English Language, "prescription" can refer to:

- The act of laying down authoritative directions.
- The establishment of rules of conduct.
- The issuance of medical directives.

In the context of this book, 'prescription' is used figuratively to symbolize God's divine guidance and authoritative direction for wealth creation. It signifies the principles, strategies, and insights provided by God to facilitate financial prosperity and well-being. This divine prescription is not a set of rigid rules but a framework of wisdom, a guide to aligning our actions with God's intentions.

It is important to understand that God's prescription is not a guarantee of instant wealth but a pathway to sustainable prosperity. It requires adherence to divine principles, diligent effort, and unwavering faith. The prescription is not a one-size-fits-all formula but a personalized guide, tailored to each individual's unique gifts, talents, and circumstances.

This prescription is not limited to the financial aspect of life, but also encompasses moral and ethical conduct. To follow the divine prescription, one must also follow the divine moral code.

Wealth

The word **"wealth"** originates from Middle English "wele" or "welthe," which evolved from the Old English term "wela" (meaning prosperity, well-being, or happiness). This, in turn, is related to the Old English "wel" (meaning "well" or "in a state of good fortune").

The root "wela" is connected to the Proto-Germanic "welōn," which conveys the idea of "wish" or "desire." This suggests that true wealth is not merely about material riches but about living in accordance with one's wishes—having the means, health, and freedom to flourish.

Thus, wealth, in its deepest sense, represents:

1. Well-being – A state of health, happiness, and security.
2. Abundance – The capacity to meet needs and pursue meaningful goals.
3. Empowerment – The ability to shape one's life according to purpose and desire.

This original meaning aligns with the biblical and philosophical view of wealth—not as mere accumulation, but as stewardship, fulfillment, and the ability to bless others.

In contemporary society, wealth is often narrowly defined in monetary terms, equating it with the accumulation of material possessions. However, a more holistic understanding of wealth encompasses a broader spectrum of well-being, including:

- Financial security and abundance.
- Physical and mental health.
- Meaningful relationships.
- Personal fulfillment and purpose.
- Spiritual connection.

True wealth is not merely about accumulating riches but about cultivating a life of abundance in all its facets. It is about having the resources and capacity to live a life of purpose, contribute to society, and experience joy and fulfillment.

Wealth, as defined in this book, is not a selfish pursuit but a means to empower others and contribute to the collective good. It is about creating an environment where individuals can thrive, reach their full potential, and experience a state of well-being.

Correlation Between Wealth and Work

The relationship between wealth and work is interdependent, a fundamental principle deeply rooted into the fabric of creation. Wealth does not materialize in a vacuum; it is the fruit of labor, the tangible outcome of purposeful activity. The principle of sowing and reaping, a cornerstone of divine wisdom, highlights this intrinsic connection. **"Bake your bread before you can eat it."** This simple adage expresses the essence of this principle. Without sowing, there can be no harvest; without labor, there can be no prosperity. God does not bestow wealth upon those who remain idle; He empowers those who diligently engage in productive work.

> ***"But remember the Lord your God, for it is He who gives you the ability to produce wealth..." (Deuteronomy 8:18).*** This verse highlights the divine source of our capacity to create wealth. God grants us the ability, but it is our responsibility to utilize it effectively. The choices we make, the actions we take, determine whether we transform this potential into tangible prosperity.

The Wealth Creation Equation

Your work + God's blessing = Wealth

This equation expresses the essence of wealth creation, highlighting the interplay between human effort and divine favor. However, it is crucial to recognize that this equation is not merely a mathematical formula; it is a dynamic process that requires integrity, faith, and a deep reverence for God.

> The story of Isaac, as recounted in Genesis 26:12-14, ***"Then Isaac sowed in that land, and reaped in the same year a hundredfold; and the LORD blessed him. The man began to prosper, and continued prospering until he became very prosperous; for he had possessions of flocks and possessions of herds and a great number of servants. So the Philistines envied him."*** exemplifies this principle. Isaac's diligent labor, coupled with God's blessing, resulted in an abundant harvest and extraordinary prosperity. This narrative highlights the importance of both human effort and divine favor in the creation of wealth.

Wealth Creation

In the context of this book, wealth creation extends beyond the accumulation of personal riches; it encompasses the ability to create an enabling environment for others to achieve a state of well-being. It is about generating opportunities, providing resources, and fostering a culture of prosperity.

True wealth creation is a selfless endeavor, a commitment to making a positive impact on the lives of others. It is about using our resources and influence to uplift communities, empower individuals, and contribute to the advancement of society.

Why a Prescription?

God's desire for humanity is one of abundance and well-being. He created us in His image, endowed us with potential, and entrusted us with the stewardship of the earth. His prescription for wealth creation is rooted in this divine intention, a pathway to experiencing the fullness of life.

> ***"Beloved, I pray that you may prosper in all things and be in health, just as your soul prospers" (3 John 2).*** This verse highlights God's desire for our holistic well-being, encompassing both physical and spiritual prosperity.

Failure to align our lives with God's will results in a state of "dis-ease," a lack of ease and well-being. This dis-ease manifests as poverty, a condition characterized by a lack of diligence and purposeful activity.

> ***"Lazy hands make a man poor, but diligent hands bring wealth" (Proverbs 10:4).*** This proverb highlights the direct correlation between diligence and prosperity, highlighting the importance of work in God's prescription for wealth creation.

God's will for us is to be wealthy, and He directs us to work because our sustenance comes through work. Failure to work results in poverty.

> ***"If a man will not work, he shall not eat" (2 Thessalonians 3:10).*** This verse emphasizes the fundamental principle that work is

> essential for sustenance.

Work was never meant to be toilsome and a burden but a blessing and a key to many pleasures.

Poverty robs you of your voice and dignity. Work is the only preventive and curative measure against it. You can prevent and cure poverty through work.

> ***"Now there was found in that city a poor man, and he by his wisdom delivered the city. Yet no one remembered that same poor man. Then I said, wisdom is better than strength. Nevertheless, the poor man's wisdom is despised, and his words are not heard" (Ecclesiastes 9:15-16).***
>
> ***"Work is the grand cure for all the maladies and miseries that ever beset mankind" (Thomas Carlyle).***

Poverty is the true definition of hell. To experience hell, look for poverty. It strips individuals of their dignity, voice, and potential. Wealth creation, therefore, is not just a financial pursuit but a means to restore dignity, empower individuals, and uplift communities.

What This Book Is About

This book aims to provide a comprehensive guide to understanding and appreciating the significance of work in relation to wealth creation. It is not a get-rich-quick scheme but a pathway to sustainable prosperity, a journey of personal transformation and societal contribution.

The principles and strategies outlined in this book are intended to provoke you into becoming the best version of yourself, so you can help others achieve the same. It is a call to action, an invitation to embrace your potential and contribute to the flourishing of humanity.

I

PART A: The Divine Blueprint for Wealth Creation

To truly flourish, one must first grasp the broader context of their existence and surroundings. Without this fundamental understanding, one risks a life of unfulfilled potential and misdirected effort. To navigate life's complexities and discover one's purpose, it is essential to comprehend the environment in which we operate. It is through this understanding that we discern the needs of our world and identify the unique role we are called to play.

1

THE DIVINE BLUEPRINT FOR WEALTH:THE POWER OF WORK

The fundamental understanding that God is the creator of the universe, and that man is entrusted as steward and custodian of the earth, sets the stage for a life of purpose, responsibility, and impactful contribution. This divine mandate, this sacred trust, positions us not as passive inhabitants, but as active participants in the ongoing unfolding of creation. We are called to cultivate, to nurture, and to enhance the world around us, recognizing that our actions have consequences that extend beyond our own individual lives.

This stewardship is not merely about preserving the natural environment, although that is certainly a vital aspect. It also encompasses the responsible use of our talents, the ethical application of our knowledge in driving progress, and the compassionate engagement with our fellow human beings.

The true measure of success, therefore, is not found in the accumulation of personal wealth or the attainment of individual accolades. It is found in the positive impact we have on the lives of others, in the tangible difference we make in our communities, and in the lasting legacy we leave behind. You are not truly successful until you have made the lives of other people in your environment better than you found them. This principle highlights the importance of service, the understanding that our own well-being is deeply connected to the well-being of those around us.

In this context, "**work**" means much more than just a job to get money. It's seen as a crucial tool for living a full life here on Earth. Through meaningful work, we get to use our skills and ideas, find our sense of purpose, and help make the world a better place. That's usually how we bring about good things and make our individual mark.

In simpler terms: Work isn't just about a paycheck; it's a key way we survive and thrive, express ourselves, find our purpose, and contribute something good to the world, leaving our mark.

God has provided us with the earth as a blank canvas, a vast expanse of potential waiting to be shaped and molded. Our lives are the pen, the instrument of creation, and the unique gifts we possess are the ink, the vibrant colors that bring our vision to life. Putting pen to paper, engaging in meaningful work, is the act of creation, the process of transforming our potential into tangible results.

The question that echoes through time, the question that challenges us to consider our legacy, is this: what legacy will you leave for others to see and read for impact and progress in their generation? What story will your life tell? What contributions will you make? What mark will you leave on the world?

This question finds its roots in the ancient narrative of Genesis 2:15:

> ***"The LORD God took the man and put him in the Garden of Eden to work it and take care of it."***

This passage highlights the inherent connection between humanity, work, and stewardship. God placed Adam in the garden not as a mere observer, but as an active participant, entrusting him with the responsibility to cultivate and care for the world around him.

This mandate extends to each and every one of us. We are all called to be gardeners, to cultivate the potential that surrounds us, to nurture the seeds of innovation, and to create a world that is more beautiful, more just, and more fulfilling than the one we inherited.

Our legacy is not defined by the material possessions we accumulate, but by the lives we touch, the communities we build, and the positive impact we make on the world. It is about using our gifts and talents to create opportunities for others, to solve problems, and to leave a lasting legacy of hope and inspiration.

It is about understanding that our lives are not isolated events, but interconnected threads in the grand design of humanity. Our actions have consequences that ripple through time, affecting generations to come.

The Foundation of Abundance: God's Design

God's creation of humanity was an act of profound love and intentionality. We were not brought forth to languish in scarcity, nor to succumb to the shadows of hopelessness. Instead, we were conceived to blossom in a realm of overflowing abundance, to mirror the very essence of the divine within us. This reflection, this vibrant expression of our created nature, is firmly tied to a life of profound joy. And this joy, in its most fundamental form, is nurtured by the secure fulfillment of our basic, human needs.

When these needs are left wanting, when the bedrock of our existence is shaken by deprivation, a sense of inadequacy takes root, casting a long shadow over our self-perception. This deficiency, this feeling of being less than whole, can lead to a series of psychological and emotional distress, eroding our sense of well-being. Poverty, in particular, is not merely a state of financial lack; it is a profound "**dis-ease**," a condition that disrupts the harmony of our lives and impedes our capacity for true flourishing. It's like an inner conflict that spreads through every part of who we are, stopping us from living the life we were meant to live.

God's original plan, the very blueprint of humanity's existence, was a life brimming with abundance, a reality where our essential needs are met with ease, and joy permeates every corner of our experience. This isn't a pipe dream or an impractical ideal. It's a real, God-given possibility that's actually built into the world around us, and it works according to dependable, unchanging principles. Just think about the incredible way God created everything, the careful attention he gave during those initial six days. He didn't just haphazardly assemble the earth; he thoughtfully formed it, filling it with beauty and all the resources we'd need, before he even made us. The key thing to grasp is that God always intended for us to have an abundance. He deeply desires that we experience a truly full life – one marked by peace, prosperity, and a sense of meaning. This was not a random act, but a deliberate, purposeful plan, a great design to crown humanity with dominion and joy, to elevate us to a position of stewardship and fulfillment.

The words of Psalm 8:4-6 bring to light the awe-inspiring truth of God's regard for humanity:

> ***"What is man that you are mindful of him, and the son of man that you visit him? For you have made him a little lower than the angels and crowned him with glory and honor. You have given him dominion over the works of your hands; you have put all things under his feet."***

This passage reveals the depth of God's affection for us, the high esteem in which He holds us. He has not only created us, but He has bestowed upon us a position of honor and authority, granting us dominion over the works of His hands. This elevated position is not meant for mere personal enjoyment but is closely linked to a life of purpose and contribution.

The apostle Paul, in his letter to the Corinthians, further illuminates the interconnectedness of God's provision, abundance, and good works. He writes,

> ***"so that in all things at all times, having all that you need, you will abound in every good work." - 2 Corinthians 9:8***

This verse highlights the divine intention for our lives: not merely to survive, but to thrive, to experience abundance in every area of our existence. This abundance, however, is not meant for selfish indulgence. It is intended to empower us to engage in "**every good work**," to become instruments of God's love and grace in the world.

God's careful preparation of the earth before placing humanity within it was not a mere coincidence. It was a deliberate act of provision, a testament to His unwavering commitment to our well-being. He designed the world to be a place where our needs would be met, where we would have access to the resources necessary to flourish. This provision, however, is not merely about material possessions. It encompasses every aspect of our lives: our physical health, our emotional well-being, our spiritual growth, and our relationships with others.

The abundant life God designed for us isn't something we just wait for; it's an active invitation to engage with. It is a call to partner with Him in the creation of a life filled with purpose and prosperity. It is a call to embrace the principles that govern abundance, to cultivate a mindset of gratitude and generosity, and to use our gifts and resources to bless others. When we align ourselves with God's design, we open ourselves to the flow of His provision, experiencing the fullness of life that He intended for us from the very beginning.

The Principle of Responsibility: Work as Cultivation

God's plan for us includes endless joy and abundance. But this isn't something we just receive without effort. Instead, we actively create this joy by following His divine principles. The foremost of these principles is personal responsibility.

> ***"God gives every bird its food, but He does not throw it into the nest." – Anonymous.***

This simple, yet profound, analogy beautifully illustrates the essence of our role in the great design of creation. It highlights the vital importance of active participation, of engaging with the world around us, in order to meet our needs and fulfill our potential. From the very dawn of humanity, our mandate has been clear: to cultivate the earth, to work it with diligence and purpose, and to draw forth its natural bounty. The earth, in its infinite generosity, holds within its depths everything necessary for life, for sustenance, and for flourishing. Our role, our sacred responsibility, is to unlock this potential, to transform the raw materials of creation into the tangible fruits of our labor.

The wisdom of Proverbs 28:19 echoes this truth:

> ***"He who works his land will have abundant food, but the one who chases fantasies will have his fill of poverty."***

This verse speaks to the fundamental connection between effort and reward. It highlights the stark contrast between those who engage in productive labor and those who chase fleeting illusions. The former, through their diligent work, reap a harvest of abundance, while the latter, driven by empty desires, find themselves trapped in a cycle of poverty and disillusionment.

Psalm 104:14-15 paints a vivid picture of God's provision and the role of human cultivation:

> ***"He makes grass grow for the cattle, and plants for people to cultivate—bringing forth food from the earth: wine that gladdens human hearts, oil to make their faces shine, and bread that sustains human lives."***

This passage reveals the delicate balance between divine provision and human agency. God, in His infinite wisdom, provides the raw materials, the seeds of life, but it is through our cultivation, our active participation, that these seeds blossom into the sustenance that nourishes and sustains us.

Understanding Your Environment: The Foundation of Flourishing

To truly flourish, one must first grasp the broader context of their existence and surroundings. Without this fundamental understanding, one risks a life of unfulfilled potential and misdirected effort. To navigate life's complexities and discover one's purpose, it is essential to comprehend the environment in which we operate. It is through this understanding that we discern the needs of our world and identify the unique role we are called to play.

This principle finds its roots in a biblical worldview, where the creation narrative establishes a foundational framework for human endeavor. God, the creator of the universe, entrusted humanity with stewardship over the earth, a responsibility that necessitates understanding and engagement with the world around us. This divine mandate implies that our purpose is not merely to exist, but to actively participate in the ongoing unfolding of creation, using our gifts and talents to cultivate, enhance, and contribute to the world.

By understanding the environment, we gain insight into the specific needs and challenges that exist. We recognize the opportunities for innovation, the potential for service, and the pathways for contribution. This understanding informs our purpose, guiding us toward meaningful work and impactful action. It is through this lens that we can discern the problems that require solutions, the needs that demand attention, and the opportunities that beckon us to create value.

Work: A Sacred Act and Partnership with the Divine

Work, therefore, is not merely a means of survival, a necessary chore to be endured. It is a sacred act, a partnership with the divine, a key that unlocks the hidden treasures within the earth and the boundless blessings of God. It is through our labor, our diligent application of our God-given talents and abilities, that we manifest the abundance that God has ordained for us. This diligent application of our abilities extends beyond physical labor to the realm of intellectual and spiritual exploration.

Proverbs 25:2 further illuminates the relationship between God's hidden wisdom and humanity's quest for understanding:

> ***"It is the glory of God to conceal a matter; but the glory of kings is to search out a matter."***

This verse speaks to the dynamic interplay between divine revelation and human exploration. God, in His infinite wisdom, conceals profound truths within the fabric of creation, inviting us to embark on a journey of discovery. It is through our diligent search, our relentless pursuit of knowledge and understanding, that we uncover these hidden treasures and unlock the secrets of abundance.

Therefore, this principle of responsibility, encompassing both physical and intellectual effort is not a burden, but a privilege. It is an invitation to participate in the ongoing creation, to become co-creators with God, to shape our destinies and to contribute to the flourishing of the world around us. It is a call to embrace our God-given potential, to cultivate our talents, and to use our abilities to create a life of abundance, not only for ourselves, but for generations to come.

This principle extends far beyond the realm of physical labor. It encompasses every aspect of our lives: our relationships, our finances, our health, and our spiritual growth. We are responsible for cultivating healthy relationships, for managing our resources wisely, for taking care of our bodies, and for nurturing our souls. By embracing this principle of responsibility, we align ourselves with God's design, becoming stewards of His creation and partners in His plan for abundance.

The seed of abundance is planted within each of us, waiting to be cultivated through responsible action. It is through our diligent labor, our unwavering commitment to our God-given purpose, that this seed blossoms into a harvest of joy, prosperity, and lasting fulfillment. Let us embrace the principle of responsibility, not as a burden, but as a gateway to the abundant life that God has ordained for us.

Defining Work: Beyond Physical Exertion

Work, as a concept, goes beyond mere physical exertion. It encompasses any purposeful activity, whether intellectual or physical, that adds value to one's own life and the lives of others. It involves the utilization of our talents and gifts to contribute to the well-being of society.

Work is the means by which we manifest our inner potential and gain substance. It is a God-ordained activity, a fundamental aspect of humanity's purpose from the very beginning. (See Genesis 2:15).

Work was originally intended as a blessing, a source of joy and fulfillment. However, the introduction of sin distorted this pattern, transforming work into a burden, a toilsome activity to be endured.

> ***"To Adam he said, "Because you listened to your wife and ate fruit from the tree about which I commanded you, 'You must not eat from it,' cursed is the ground because of you; through painful toil you will eat food from it all the days of your life. It will produce thorns and thistles for you, and you will eat the plants of the field. By the sweat of your brow you will eat your food until you return to the ground..." - Genesis 3:17-19***

Sin transformed work from a blessing into a perceived burden, tempting many to seek unearned wealth. However, genuine and enduring prosperity stems from "**created wealth**," the result of diligent labor and purposeful activity.

> ***"Dishonest money dwindles, but whoever gathers little by little makes it grow." - Proverbs 13:11***
> ***"Like a partridge that hatches eggs it did not lay, so are those who gain riches by unjust means. When their lives are half over, their riches will desert them, and in the end they will prove to be fools." - Jeremiah 17:11***

Work is a sanctified activity, redeemed through God's grace and transformed back into a blessing. The ground is no longer cursed, and work is once again a means of blessing and fulfillment.

> ***"When the LORD smelled the pleasing aroma, he said in his heart: "Never again will I curse the ground because of humans... As long as the earth endures, seedtime and harvest, cold and heat,***

> ***summer and winter, day and night will never cease." - Genesis 8:21-22***

Therefore, idleness is contrary to God's design. God desires us to live joyful and vibrant lives, and work is an essential component of this joy. If we truly love and fear God, we will fear idleness.

> ***"Anyone who has been stealing must steal no longer, but must work, doing something useful with their own hands, so that they may have something to share with those in need." - Ephesians 4:28***

Work fosters independence, while idleness leads to dependence and shame.

> ***"Make it your ambition to lead a quiet life: You should mind your own business and work with your hands... so that your daily life may win the respect of outsiders and so that you may not be dependent on anybody." - 1 Thessalonians 4:11-12***

Shunning work leads to poverty.

> ***"Whoever loves pleasure will become poor; whoever loves wine and olive oil will never be rich." - Proverbs 21:17***

Work as a Process: The Power of Small Beginnings

Work, as a key to wealth creation, is a process, not a singular event. It has a beginning, and this beginning is often small. Many people avoid work because they despise small beginnings, fixated on instant success.

However, small beginnings are the foundation of great achievements.

> ***"Though your beginning was small, yet your latter end would increase abundantly." - Job 8:7***

The story of Elijah and the small cloud serves as a powerful illustration of this principle.

> ***"The seventh time the servant reported, "A cloud as small as a man's hand is rising from the sea." So Elijah said, "Go and tell Ahab, 'Hitch up your chariot and go down, so the rain doesn't stop you.'" Meanwhile, the sky grew dark with clouds and wind, and a heavy rain came on." - 1 Kings 18:44-45***

Just as the small cloud heralded a great rain, the ability to recognize and act upon small opportunities is crucial in business and entrepreneurship.

> ***"The testing of an entrepreneur is in the ability to start the process of wealth creation from humble beginnings. Identifying business opportunities requires humility." - Chibamba Kanyama, Business Post.***

Therefore, cultivating a positive attitude toward small beginnings, coupled with faithful responsibility, paves the way to true greatness. Your progress in life is largely determined by how you handle small beginnings and demonstrate responsibility.

> ***"Well done, good and faithful servant; you were faithful over a few things, I will make you ruler over many things." - Matthew 25:23.***

A positive attitude toward small beginnings is key to greatness.

Manifesting Potential and Purpose

The human experience is fundamentally linked to purpose. To live a life devoid of meaningful work is to exist in a state of unfulfilled potential, a condition that breeds frustration and discontent. The most profound source of frustration is the awareness of untapped potential, the feeling of being a burden to oneself and society. Humans are created with an innate drive to contribute, to create, and to leave a lasting impact.

Work, in its truest form, is the very conduit through which we unleash this natural potential. It is the vital valve that regulates the flow of our God-given abilities, transforming dormant talents into tangible contributions that enrich our lives and the lives of those around us. Engaging in meaningful work means you're actively showing what you were meant to do. It's about bringing out that special mix of talents and abilities that you have deep inside. It is the act of transforming the abstract into the concrete, the dream into reality. When our potential is fully realized, when the wellspring of our abilities flows freely, a profound sense of satisfaction and fulfillment permeates every aspect of our existence, coloring our experiences with a deep and abiding joy.

The pursuit of God's kingdom, as articulated in Matthew 6:33, is not merely a spiritual endeavor confined to the realm of the spiritual. It is, in essence, the pursuit of maximizing one's potential, a holistic approach to life that encompasses the development and utilization of our God-given abilities. It is the understanding that our talents are not meant to be buried, but to be cultivated and shared with the world.

Seeking God's kingdom is about aligning our lives with His purpose, about becoming the people He created us to be, and about using our gifts to contribute to the betterment of humanity.

Maximizing our potential is the path to true wealth, a wealth that goes beyond the temporary attraction of material possessions. It is a wealth that encompasses a life of purpose and impact, a life that is filled with meaning and fulfillment. It is the understanding that our greatest treasures are not found in bank accounts or stock portfolios, but in the intangible riches of our character, our relationships, and our contributions to the world.

To embrace work as a sacred act is to understand that it is not merely about earning a living, but about living a life of purpose. It is about recognizing that our work is an expression of our creativity, a manifestation of our love, and a testament to our commitment to making a difference. It is about understanding that our work is not separate from our faith, but an integral part of it, a way to honor God and to serve others.

When we approach work with this understanding, we transform it from a chore into a calling, from a burden into a blessing. We find joy in our labor, satisfaction in our accomplishments, and a deep sense of purpose in our contributions. We understand that our work is not merely about what we do, but about who we are becoming. It is about shaping our character, developing our skills, and growing in wisdom and understanding.

The human experience is a complex composition of potential, waiting to be guided by the power of meaningful work. Let's embrace work not as a tiresome chore, but as a sacred invitation. It's our chance to show our purpose, to unleash our full potential, and to build a life that truly matters. We should work, not just to be busy, but to grow into the people God wants us to be, to help humanity thrive, and to create a legacy that lasts forever.

Internal Drive and Divine Assignment

> ***"Enterprise is an in-born, natural capacity that requires simple engagement in a reasonable activity." - Chibamba Kanyama, Business Post.***

Starting your unique work isn't about waiting for others to give you permission or a task. Instead, it's an inner drive, a divine calling that comes from deep inside you. No one but God can give you the work that is truly yours. The fact that you exist at all proves your purpose and shows you have a special role to play in life's grand plan.

Your conception, birth, and continued existence are evidence of a divine assignment. You are here for a reason, and you have work to do. The key is to understand your motivation, figure out the purpose behind your actions, and then commit to working as hard as you can.

> ***"It is appointed for man to die once, and after that comes judgment." - Hebrews 9:27***

At the end of your life, you will be held accountable for what you did, or failed to do, with the gifts and opportunities entrusted to you.

> ***"No man is born into this world whose work is not born with him." - J.R. Lowell.***

The lie perpetuated by the adversary is that you must wait for someone to employ you before you can engage in meaningful work and realize your substance. This deception is the root of idleness and unproductive living, particularly during periods of unemployment. However, the absence of employment does not equate to the absence of work.

Work is a broader concept, transcending the limitations of traditional employment.

Employment is an external arrangement, a contractual agreement between an individual and an organization. Work, on the other hand, is an internal drive, an intrinsic aspect of your being. Employment is detached from your essence, while work is an expression of your very life. It is through your work, not merely your employment, that the world will recognize your value and leaders will seek your counsel.

Unemployment often stems from an unwillingness to engage in meaningful work. The fewer individuals who are willing to work, the fewer opportunities for employment are created, leading to a higher unemployment rate. Work is the catalyst for employment creation; it is the seed that germinates into job opportunities.

Only God can truly assign you the work that aligns with your purpose, for only He knows the depths of your potential. Others may offer jobs or employment, hoping that you will fulfill their expectations. However, not everyone who is employed is truly engaged in meaningful work. The prevalence of terms like "**retrenchment**" and "**downsizing**" is a testament to the prevalence of unproductive labor.

Do not be content with merely being employed. Strive to engage in meaningful work, to manifest your potential, and to be productively effective. Let your work earn you employment, rather than relying on employment to define your work.

Employment is not synonymous with work; rather, work is the pathway to meaningful employment.

Do not be satisfied with the security of a salary alone. While a salary is a valuable form of compensation, it is not the source of true fulfillment. True satisfaction comes from engaging in meaningful work, from manifesting your potential, and from contributing to the well-being of others. A salary is a secondary consideration, a byproduct of diligent and purposeful work. It is diligent work that sustains and defines you, not merely a paycheck.

> ***"The hand of the diligent will rule, but the lazy man will be put to forced labor." - Proverbs 12:24.***
> ***"From the fruit of their mouth a person's stomach will be filled; with the harvest of their hands they will be rewarded." - Proverbs 12:14.***

It is not employment that rewards you; it is the work you perform. Employment and salary can be taken away, but your work, your inherent abilities, cannot. Those who understand the principles of work will be sustained in all seasons, regardless of external circumstances. Your work is an integral part of your being, an expression of who you are. Because of your work, others will seek you out, bringing gifts and opportunities.

> ***"When the queen of Sheba heard about the fame of Solomon and his relation to the name of the Lord, she came to test him with hard questions... She gave the king 120 talents of gold, large quantities of spices, and precious stones. Never again were so many spices brought in as those the queen of Sheba gave to King Solomon." - 1 Kings 10:1-2, 10.***

True wealth is not attained by chasing money; it is achieved by maximizing your potential and fulfilling your purpose.

Unwrapping Your Potential

God has equipped you for success because you are inherently gifted.

> ***"For we are God's handiwork, created in Christ Jesus to do good works, which God prepared in advance for us to do." - Ephesians 2:10.***

Every individual is born with a God-ordained gift, a potential for greatness. This gift is what distinguishes you, what makes you valuable and recognizable. It is your passport to success, revealed through your work. Others will only recognize your gift when they witness your work.

> ***"Let your light shine before others, that they may see your good deeds and glorify your Father in heaven." - Matthew 5:16.***
> ***"A gift opens the way for the giver and ushers him into the presence of the great." - Proverbs 18:16.***

"**What God has given you is the secret to what God has promised you.**" **- Dr. Mike Murdock.**

You are a gift box, containing a treasure trove of potential. However, the gift remains hidden until you unwrap it, until you manifest your abilities through work. As long as the gift remains wrapped, the world cannot benefit from your unique contributions. The world needs you, but it can only appreciate you when your inner potential is visible.

Unwrap yourself by engaging in meaningful work, by manifesting your potential. Put yourself to work, reveal your gift, and abundance will follow. The world awaits the working of your gift.

You are known by your work. A craftsman is recognized by the quality of his craft. Even when seeking employment, employers assess your work value, reviewing your resume or CV to determine your past accomplishments.

To claim you have no experience because you have never been employed is a self-defeating mindset. You are not employed merely because you need a job; you are employed because you have a proven track record of demonstrating your abilities.

You are not given employment so you can work; you are employed because you already work. Value is not based on appearance or credentials; it is based on what you can do, on your demonstrated abilities. Work value is purpose value. When you engage in meaningful work, employment will seek you out. And when you work, you will have the power to command and choose employment on your terms.

Work is not merely what you do when you are employed; it is what you do because you are you. It is an expression of your identity, your purpose, your calling. Get busy now, and work out the potential that resides within you. The world is waiting for your contribution.

A Call to Action: Cultivate Your Divine Potential

Therefore, let us not be passive recipients of God's blessings, but active participants in His grand design. Embrace your role as a steward of the earth and your unique talents. Cultivate your gifts with diligence, work with purpose, and contribute generously to the lives of others. Your journey to true wealth and lasting impact begins with the conscious choice to act, to transform potential into reality, and to leave a legacy that echoes God's abundant love for generations to come. What step will you take today to cultivate your divine potential and create a lasting impact?

II

PART B: The Awakening to Potential

The journey to success begins with a profound realization: that within each individual lies the capacity for extraordinary achievement. This isn't just a quick idea; it's a deep change in how you see yourself, acknowledging the inner strength and control you truly possess. It is the understanding that the seeds of success are sown within, and that personal responsibility is the fertile ground in which they grow.

2

THE SUCCESS EQUATION

Success, often perceived as a singular achievement, is in reality a delicate balance, a harmonious interplay between two fundamental forces: responsibility and authority. The equation that expresses this relationship is:

Responsibility + Authority = Dominion (Success)

This chapter will primarily focus on responsibility, the cornerstone of true success, as authority naturally arises from the effective demonstration of responsibility. While authority, the right to exercise power over a specific sphere of influence, is a vital component, it is responsibility that lays the groundwork for its acquisition and sustenance.

The Primacy of Responsibility

Authority, in many instances, is a more static factor, a given right or position. It is a title, a designation, a place on the organizational chart. But while it might give you a platform, it's responsibility that builds the foundation for real influence and lasting success. Your ability to genuinely shape your environment and make a meaningful impact is directly linked to how much responsibility you show. True success isn't just handed to you; you carefully build it by consistently and diligently taking responsibility in whatever you do.

At its core, responsibility embodies accountability. It's your ability to respond effectively, thoughtfully, and proactively to the many situations that arise in your life and surroundings. This responsiveness, this proven capacity to act with purpose and integrity, truly measures your authority, leadership, and adaptability. While titles or positions might grant you authority, responsibility is a self-determined choice, an inner guide shaping your actions and character. Your environment—be it your workplace, community, or family—grants you genuine authority, the power to influence and create change, in direct proportion to the responsibility you demonstrate. It's not about demanding respect; it's about earning it through consistent, reliable actions.

Think of a garden: the gardener might have the title of "owner," but it's their consistent responsibility—watering, weeding, nurturing—that brings the garden to life. Without that effort, the title means nothing. Similarly, a leader might hold a position, but without the responsibility to guide, support, and empower their team, their authority quickly fades.

Moreover, responsibility dictates your life's productivity and profitability, not just financially, but in your overall well-being and fulfillment. It's the driving force behind your actions, the catalyst for your achievements. It's the understanding that you're not a passive recipient of circumstances, but an active agent in shaping your destiny. Responsibility empowers you to own your choices, learn from your mistakes, and constantly strive for improvement.

Responsibility isn't a burden to avoid; it's a privilege to embrace. It's knowing you have the power to make a difference, contribute to the world, and create a life of meaning and purpose. It's recognizing that your actions have consequences, your choices matter, and you're accountable for the impact you have on others.

To cultivate responsibility is to cultivate integrity, develop a strong moral compass, and build a reputation for reliability and trustworthiness. It's understanding that true leadership isn't about controlling others, but about empowering them, serving their needs, and creating an environment where they can thrive.

Ultimately, responsibility is the bedrock upon which all lasting success is built. It's the cornerstone of influence, the foundation of achievement, and the key to unlocking your full potential. It's not about waiting for permission to act, but about taking initiative, stepping up, and making a positive impact on the world. By embracing the primacy of responsibility, you become the architect of your own influence, building a legacy of integrity, achievement, and lasting significance.

The Self-Confrontation of Responsibility

Living a purposeful and fulfilling life starts with an honest confrontation with yourself. It's a deep moment of self-reflection where you truly acknowledge the power and importance of your own choices.

While we can delegate tasks, distribute assignments, and seek help from others, the fundamental essence of responsibility remains non-transferable. At our core, we are the ultimate architects of our own destinies, the sole owners of our actions and their consequences. We're accountable for the outcomes our choices create, for fulfilling the duties we embrace, and for the legacy we leave behind.

Life, with its complex design of challenges and opportunities, often presents us with numerous obstacles and a landscape shrouded in uncertainty. Yet, amidst this ever-shifting terrain, one unwavering truth remains: only we possess the power to overcome the hurdles in our path. Others might offer a helping hand, guidance, and unwavering support, but the ultimate responsibility for charting our life's trajectory, for navigating storms and embracing sunshine, rests squarely on our shoulders. It's our internal compass, our moral compass, that must guide us through life's complexities.

Responsibility isn't passively accepting circumstances; it's an active, conscious engagement in improving our lives and enhancing our surroundings. It's the awakening of our minds and the sharpening of our perceptions, a profound "coming to our senses"—a moment of clarity where we recognize our agency and embrace our capacity for change. The parable of the prodigal son, as recounted in Luke 15:17-20, powerfully illustrates this transformative self-confrontation:

> ***"When he came to his senses, he said, 'How many of my father's hired servants have food to spare, and here I am starving to death! I will set out and go back to my father and say to him: Father, I have sinned against heaven and against you. I am no longer worthy to be called your son; make me like one of your hired servants.' So he got up and went to his father."***

The prodigal son's journey mirrors a version of the human experience, reflecting our tendency to stray from our true path, squander potential, and succumb to fleeting pleasures. However, his moment of **"coming to his senses"** marks a pivotal turning point—a recognition of his own responsibility for his predicament and a decision to act. He confronts the reality of his situation, acknowledges his mistakes, and chooses to return to the path of righteousness.

This self-confrontation, this honest introspection, is the crucible where responsibility is forged. It's the understanding that we aren't victims of circumstance, but active agents in shaping our lives. It's the recognition that we have the power to choose, to change, and to create a better future.

Therefore, responsibility isn't a burden to be feared, but a privilege to embrace. It's the key that unlocks our potential, the compass that guides our journey, and the foundation upon which we build a life of purpose and fulfillment. It's the understanding that we are accountable not only to ourselves, but to the world around us, to the people whose lives we touch, and to the legacy we leave behind.

To embrace the self-confrontation of responsibility is to embark on a journey of continuous growth—a path of self-discovery where we learn from mistakes, cultivate strengths, and strive to become our best selves. It's the understanding that our lives aren't predetermined, but malleable, capable of being shaped by our choices and actions. It's the recognition that we have the power to create a life of meaning, purpose, and lasting significance.

Response-Ability: The Measure of Success

Think of responsibility as **"response-ability"**—your ability to respond positively and effectively to life's situations. Your success directly relates to this **"response-ability,"** your capacity to meet life's demands. Consequently, where there's responsibility, accountability inevitably follows. **"Account-ability"** is your ability to account for your responsibility, an assessment of how you used the talents and opportunities given to you.

This interconnectedness is vividly illustrated in the parable of the talents in Matthew 25:14-30. In this story, the master gives his servants different sums of money—**"talents"**—placing a clear responsibility on each to manage and grow what they've received. Upon his return, he doesn't just ask about the outcome; he holds each servant accountable for how they used their responsibility in handling his resources. The servants who embraced their responsibility by diligently investing and increasing their talents were praised and rewarded for their proactive engagement. In stark contrast, the servant who avoided his responsibility by burying his talent out of fear faced rebuke and the loss of his entrusted sum because of his failure to act responsibly. Similarly, in your own life, you'll be held accountable for how you lived it—for whether you actively took responsibility to add value to your environment or squandered your potential with excuses and blame, much like the unfaithful servant who neglected his responsibility.

Embracing responsibility, even amidst life's most challenging circumstances, opens a pathway to fulfillment. Responsibility fosters an action plan, a strategic approach to navigating and overcoming hardship. It cultivates the understanding that no one else can fulfill your unique purpose. Your individual portion, your distinct destiny, belongs to you alone, and you're accountable for its realization. This is a direct consequence of how you choose to take responsibility for it, just as each servant in the parable was responsible for—and then held accountable for—the talents specifically entrusted to their care. Hence, the adage, **"You are the master of your destiny,"** rings true: your contribution to society is your responsibility, and you'll be held accountable for how you fulfill it. Should you choose to neglect or abandon this responsibility, you'll be held accountable for your inaction, mirroring the consequences faced by the servant who failed to take responsibility for his talent.

The Undeniable Nature of Responsibility

The concept of responsibility stands as an unwavering anchor in the turbulent sea of life, an immutable truth that cannot be shifted or compromised. You can never delegate responsibility. While the delegation of authority, the passing of tasks and duties to others, is a common practice, the fundamental essence of responsibility remains firmly rooted within the individual. You can, indeed, entrust others with the execution of specific actions, but the ultimate accountability for the outcome, the final reckoning, rests squarely upon your shoulders.

The act of delegating a task does not absolve you of the inherent responsibility for its successful completion. It is a shared endeavor, a collaborative effort, but the buck ultimately stops with you.

This principle reaches into the very essence of your existence, shaping your life's journey. When it all comes down to it, you're the chief architect of your own success. Though others—like parents, guardians, mentors, or societal figures—might have had authority over you at various stages, their performance, good or bad, doesn't set the limits of your future. Their actions, or lack thereof, don't dictate your potential. If they, for any reason, failed in their responsibilities or stumbled in their duties, it's now your responsibility to fix things, to take ownership of your life's story, and to steer it toward success.

The canvas of your life is yours to paint, the story of your existence yours to write. No one else bears more responsibility for its improvement, for its unfolding brilliance, than you do. The time to take ownership is now, in this very moment, where the potential for transformation truly lies. To avoid this responsibility, to push it off to a later date, is to give up control of your destiny, to surrender your power to whatever happens.

If you fail to grasp this fundamental truth, if you choose to keep blaming others for your perceived shortcomings, you'll inevitably find that judgment will turn against you. Those you once accused will eventually hold you accountable for your own lack of initiative, for your unwillingness to take charge of your life. The cycle of blame is a self-feeding trap, a web of excuses that leads only to stagnation and regret.

So, the command is clear: stop blaming external factors, past experiences, or the supposed failures of others. Instead, embrace the empowering reality of responsibility—the understanding that you are the master of your own destiny. Take charge of your life, develop your potential, and create a future that truly reflects your hopes and values.

This isn't about shouldering the world's burdens; it's about embracing the inherent power within you. It's a call to recognize that you're not a victim of circumstance, but a creator of your own reality. It's an invitation to step into your full potential, to use your power, and to build a life of purpose, meaning, and lasting significance.

By embracing the undeniable nature of responsibility, you free yourself from the chains of blame, the limitations of external expectations, and the paralysis of inaction. You become the captain of your own ship, the architect of your own destiny, and the author of your own story. In essence, you become the embodiment of your own potential, a testament to the transformative power of self-ownership.

The Freedom of Self-Responsibility

Self-responsibility frees you from a life of blame, unburdening you from resentment and excuses. When you let go of blame, you can see how even what an adversary meant for harm, God intended for good. What others do to you can't stop your destiny; how you respond to their actions, however, can. Be responsible. Whether life is easy or difficult, you are destined for success. You owe no one an apology for your success, only an explanation of how you achieved it.

Those who struggle to be productive, whether employed or not, often resort to blaming the government or others for their difficulties. This blame syndrome becomes a self-imposed limitation, hindering their potential. They constantly find fault in others, neglecting to address their own shortcomings, and fail to understand that blame has never solved any problem.

Consider the exchange in Genesis 3:11-13:

> ***"And he said, "Who told you that you were naked? Have you eaten from the tree that I commanded you not to eat from?" The man said, "The woman you put here with me—she gave me some fruit from the tree, and I ate it." The Lord God said to the woman, "What is this you have done?" The woman said, "The serpent deceived me, and I ate."***

When confronted by God, Adam doesn't take responsibility but points to Eve, deflecting blame. Eve, in turn, shifts the blame further to the serpent. This clearly illustrates how blame creates a chain reaction, with each person trying to avoid accountability. Importantly, this act of blaming doesn't undo their disobedience or lessen the consequences; it simply shows their unwillingness to own their choices, proving that blame is just a deflection, not a solution or a way to correct things.

As Chibamba Kanyama states in Business Post,

> ***"You are fully responsible for your success, and the community around you will merely provide enough space for you to excel. Your only limitation is yourself."***

This powerfully reinforces that your path to success is entirely your own to forge.

The Burden of Blame and the Path to Achievement

You can't achieve true success while burdened by blame. You simply can't climb the ladder of accomplishment when weighed down by excuses, nor can you see the path to success with your vision clouded by resentment, which ultimately extinguishes the flame of love within you. The challenging climb toward your goals demands clear sight, unburdened by the heavy baggage of accusations and the constant deflection of responsibility. Blame, acting like a corrosive acid, not only erodes your capacity for empathy, compassion, and collaboration but also dims the very light that guides you.

The Power of Realization

The journey to success begins with a profound realization: that within each individual lies the capacity for extraordinary achievement. This isn't just a quick idea; it's a deep change in how you see yourself, acknowledging the inner strength and control you truly possess. It is the understanding that the seeds of success are sown within, and that personal responsibility is the fertile ground in which they grow.

Realization is, in essence, a re-alignment of life to purpose. It's a moment of clarity, a turning point where one's actions begin to reflect their true potential and intended path. To realize is to recover, to reclaim the lost pieces of one's identity, to awaken to the dormant talents and untapped abilities that lie within. It is a return to self, a homecoming to one's authentic purpose.

The wisdom of Proverbs 24:30-34 illustrates the consequences of neglecting this realization. The passage depicts a scene of neglect and decay, a field overgrown with thorns and a broken-down wall, a reflection of a life lacking direction and purpose. **"When I saw it, I realized it,"** the writer reflects, **"I looked on it and received instruction."** This moment of realization serves as a stark warning against laziness and complacency, a reminder that inaction leads to poverty and hardship.

Embracing Responsibility for Meaningful Progress

Meaningful progress and the resolution of challenges only begin when you embrace the full spectrum of responsibility, acknowledging your pivotal role in both your personal advancement and the betterment of your community. This ownership of your actions and their consequences serves as the essential catalyst for transformation, igniting the spark of positive change.

Individuals who embrace self-responsibility naturally become achievers. Their solution-oriented approach is fueled by a proactive mindset that seeks understanding and resolution. They ask the crucial questions: **"What went wrong?"** and, more importantly, **"What must I do to rectify the situation?"** Rather than passively waiting for external forces to improve their circumstances, they take decisive, proactive steps to shape their desired life, determine their destiny, and contribute positively to their surroundings.

Conversely, a significant number of individuals resign themselves to lives of mediocrity, ensnared in a cycle of dependency and inaction. This stagnation arises from a fundamental lack of self-confrontation, a refusal to acknowledge their own agency and assume responsibility for their well-being. By relying on external factors to dictate their circumstances, they abdicate their power and settle for a life of unfulfilled potential. This absence of responsibility cultivates mediocrity—a state of passive acceptance—and fosters laziness—a state of inertia that actively prevents progress.

Mediocrity is a mental trap, confined by a lack of clear vision for the future, held back by outdated thinking, weakened by indecision, and stalled by procrastination. It thrives when direction is unclear, when the past dictates the present, when hesitation replaces action, and when delays become a habit. Breaking free requires clarity of purpose, forward-thinking, decisive action, and the discipline to move beyond excuses toward meaningful progress. This concise definition reveals the complex nature of mediocrity, highlighting the strong connections between what we envision, how we think, and what we actually do.

Living a Life Free from Blame

True and lasting success is attainable only when you fully embrace the weight of responsibility, consciously choosing to liberate yourself from the shackles of blame and committing to a life of proactive engagement. Strive to be an inspiration, a catalyst for positive change, a beacon of hope, rather than a source of negativity and blame. Embracing responsibility empowers others to do the same, creating a ripple effect of positive action—a chain reaction of growth and transformation.

In stark contrast, blame cripples your vision, hindering your ability to perceive the opportunities that lie ahead. It casts a dark shadow over your perception, distorting your view of reality and preventing you from recognizing the possibilities that surround you. Therefore, live a life free from blame, not only for your own personal growth but also for the sake of your vision, the dreams you cherish, and the positive impact you are capable of having on the world.

Ultimately, to live a life unburdened by blame is to embrace a life of empowerment, purpose, and lasting significance. It is to harness the power of responsibility, cultivate your natural potential, and contribute meaningfully to the flourishing of humanity.

What steps can you take today to embrace personal responsibility and move beyond blame in your own life?

The Genesis 1:28 Equation: Responsibility + Authority = Dominion

Genesis 1:28 lays the groundwork for understanding the success equation: Responsibility + Authority = Dominion (Success). God commanded humanity to be fruitful, multiply, replenish the earth, subdue it, and have dominion. These commands represent our core responsibilities.

Firstly, the mandate to be fruitful signifies our value to the world. **"Fruit,"** derived from the Latin **"fructus"** meaning **"to enjoy,"** is the reproductive product of a plant, given for enjoyment. Just as a tree is valued for its fruit, your life's work is your fruit—the tangible value you offer. The extent to which the world enjoys you is directly proportional to your fruitfulness, your capacity to bear abundant fruit, moving beyond idleness to a state of vibrant contribution.

Secondly, the call to multiply extends our impact. While the earth belongs to the Lord, we are entrusted to touch it with God's love through our gifts. These gifts, expressions of His love, gain value through our nurturing. Multiplication arises directly from fruitfulness; our work has the power to touch multitudes of lives, much like a single seed yielding abundant fruit. By manifesting our potential through work, we gain the ability to bless others, creating a positive multiplier effect that empowers the world, as Isaiah 55:5 suggests:

> ***"Surely you will summon nations you know not, and nations who do not know you will run to you."***

Thirdly, the responsibility to replenish the earth goes beyond mere physical filling. It encompasses restoring order, bringing harmony, and fulfilling our unique purpose within God's creation. This act of replenishing is intrinsically linked to multiplication. As John 12:24

profoundly states,

> ***"Unless a kernel of wheat falls to the ground and dies, it remains only a single seed. But if it dies, it produces many seeds."***

This highlights the principle that fruitfulness contains the seed for multiplication, and conversely, failing to manifest potential and multiply gifts inevitably leads to a failure to replenish one's designated sphere of influence. Furthermore, replenishing involves transforming chaos into structure, taking what is broken and making it whole, and turning barrenness into fertility.

Ultimately, you are called to actively engage with and transform the world around you. You possess the power to bring positive change, restore hope, and create a lasting legacy of impact. Your diligent fulfillment of the responsibilities to be fruitful, multiply, and replenish directly determines the scope and extent of your authority—your dominion or success in the world.

The Natural Consequence of Responsibility

When you effectively demonstrate responsibility, you bring your sphere of influence under your authority. The area you replenish becomes your territory, a domain where your influence reigns. It's in this space that you can truly exercise your gifts and fulfill your purpose.

The key to acquiring authority lies in identifying and developing your unique gift. Diligently using your potential commands authority, earning you respect and recognition. Don't chase authority; instead, let your name become synonymous with it in your field. Strive for excellence, aiming to be the best in your area of expertise.

True authority isn't about wielding power over others. It's about mastering your craft, becoming a beacon of expertise, and inspiring others through your example. It's the natural consequence of consistent responsibility, diligent effort, and an unwavering commitment to your purpose.

Subdue the Earth: Maintaining Order and Exercising Influence

Subduing the earth means maintaining order by exercising your authority. It's about bringing structure to chaos, ensuring your sphere of influence remains productive and harmonious. Here, **"earth"** represents your personal domain, a space that is limitless because your potential is unlimited.

When you consistently demonstrate responsibility, even seemingly insurmountable obstacles will submit to your influence. You'll gain the power to overcome challenges, navigate difficulties, and create a positive impact on your environment. Remember, subduing the earth isn't about dominating others; it's about mastering yourself, controlling your circumstances, and exercising your God-given authority to bring order and prosperity.

Dominion: The Ultimate Expression of Success

Dominion is the ultimate result of diligent effort, the culmination of your responsibility and authority. It is God's will for you—to prosper you, to give you hope, and to provide you with a future filled with purpose and fulfillment.

It is your responsibility to demonstrate responsibility and acquire authority. Dominion is not a distant dream, an unattainable ideal. It is a present reality, a potential that is waiting to be realized.

As John 15:8 states,

> **"This is to my Father's glory, that you bear much fruit, showing yourselves to be my disciples."**

Bearing much fruit is the evidence of your discipleship, the tangible manifestation of your commitment to God's purpose. It is through your fruitfulness, your multiplication, your replenishment, your subduing, and your dominion that you glorify God and fulfill your destiny.

Practical Applications of Responsibility and Authority

To truly grasp the power of the success equation, it's essential to understand its practical applications in everyday life.

In the Workplace:

Take ownership of your tasks and projects.

- Go beyond your job description and seek opportunities to add value.
- Be proactive in solving problems and improving processes.
- Develop your skills and expertise to become a leader in your field.
- Exercise your authority with integrity and fairness.

In Your Community:

Volunteer your time and talents to support local initiatives.

- Be a positive role model and mentor to others.
- Advocate for positive change and address community needs.
- Use your influence to promote unity and cooperation.
- Take responsibility for the well-being of your neighborhood.

In Your Family:

Be a responsible and supportive family member.

- Take initiative in creating a harmonious home environment.
- Lead by example and teach your children the importance of responsibility.
- Exercise your authority with love and wisdom.
- Be a good steward of your resources.

In Your Personal Life:

Take responsibility for your physical, emotional, and spiritual well-being.

- Set goals and develop a plan to achieve them.
- Cultivate positive habits and eliminate negative ones.
- Exercise self-discipline and control your impulses.
- Live a life of integrity and purpose.

Overcoming Obstacles to Responsibility

The path to responsibility is not always easy. There are obstacles that can hinder our progress and prevent us from fully embracing our potential.

Fear of Failure:

Fear of failure can paralyze us, preventing us from taking risks and pursuing our goals.

- Remember that failure is a learning opportunity, a stepping stone to success.
- Focus on the lessons learned from your mistakes, rather than dwelling on the negative outcomes.

Lack of Self-Confidence:

Lack of self-confidence can lead to self-doubt and inaction.

- Recognize your strengths and celebrate your accomplishments.
- Surround yourself with positive and supportive people.
- Practice positive affirmations.

Procrastination:

Procrastination is a thief of time and opportunity.

- Break down large tasks into smaller, more manageable steps.
- Set deadlines and hold yourself accountable.
- Reward yourself for completing tasks.

Blame-Shifting:

Blame-shifting is a way of avoiding responsibility.

- Take ownership of your actions and their consequences.
- Focus on solutions, rather than dwelling on problems.
- Learn from your mistakes and move forward.

By recognizing and overcoming these obstacles, you can cultivate a strong sense of responsibility and unlock your full potential.

Ultimately, the choice to embrace responsibility and exercise authority is yours. You have the power to shape your destiny, to create a life of purpose and impact. Choose to be responsible, choose to exercise your authority, and choose to fulfill your dominion.

3

VISION: THE COMPASS OF DESTINY

"Where there is no vision, the people perish." - Proverbs 29:18

"And the LORD said to Abram... 'Lift up your eyes now, and look from the place where you are—northward, southward, eastward, and westward; for all the land which you see I will give to you and to your descendants forever.'" - Genesis 13:14-15

The Indispensable Role of Vision

For someone inspired by vision, no task is too small to start, and no challenge is too big to overcome. While life is naturally rich and complex, it often feels overwhelming without clear direction. It is vision that provides this essential direction, serving as a guiding compass through life's twists and turns.

Jesus Christ, the embodiment of divine wisdom and purpose, stands as the ultimate direction—the very essence of **"the way, the truth, and the life."** He is the guiding star that illuminates our path, the unwavering beacon leading us toward our true potential. To live without direction, to wander aimlessly, is to live without devotion, for devotion is deeply linked to vision. Devotion, in its truest form, is the unwavering commitment to a cause, purpose, or person that resonates deeply within us. It is the fuel that propels us forward, sustaining us through trials and tribulations.

The absence of devotion inevitably leads to the failure to realize one's vision, as the journey toward achievement demands unwavering dedication and steadfast commitment. It is the understanding that the path may be difficult, the challenges daunting, but the ultimate reward—the fulfillment of our vision—makes every sacrifice worthwhile.

Just as direction is indispensable for devotion, it is equally essential for responsibility. Direction reveals purpose, and purpose fuels both devotion and responsibility, the twin pillars upon which a successful life is built. Without a clear understanding of our direction, we cannot truly grasp our purpose, leading to aimlessness and ineffectiveness. We become like a ship without a rudder, tossed about by the currents of circumstance, unable to reach our intended destination.

Without clear direction, you may become a **"Jack of all trades, master of none"**—a person with a wide range of skills but lacking the depth of expertise necessary to excel in any particular area. This lack of focus and specialization hinders your ability to make a meaningful impact, to contribute your unique talents to the world.

Vision, therefore, is not merely a fleeting dream or a whimsical aspiration; it is a fundamental necessity, a guiding principle that shapes our actions, directs our choices, and defines our destiny. It is the understanding that we are not merely passengers on the journey of life, but active participants, capable of shaping our own experiences and leaving a lasting legacy.

To cultivate vision is to cultivate purpose, to develop a clear understanding of our values, goals, and aspirations. It is to recognize that our lives have meaning, that we have a unique contribution to make, and that we have the power to create a better future. It is to understand that vision is not only what we see, but how we see, and that a clear vision allows us to see opportunities where others see only obstacles.

Vision provides the framework for our decisions, the lens through which we interpret our experiences, and the motivation that drives our actions. It is the guiding star that shines light upon our path, the compass that keeps us on course, and the fuel that propels us towards our ultimate destination. It is the indispensable navigator of destiny, the key that unlocks our potential and empowers us to live a life of purpose, meaning, and lasting significance.

Vision as the Starting Point

Your journey toward fulfillment begins with direction—discovering your unique course in life. Direction flows from vision. Where there's no vision, there's no direction. Where there's no direction, there's no purpose. And where there's no purpose, there's no reason for devotion or responsibility. Vision is the bedrock of direction, the guiding light that illuminates your path.

Your vision is your destination, the ultimate point of arrival, the beacon that points toward your destiny, your future, the culmination of your life's journey. Your mission, your purpose, your direction are all fundamentally connected to your destination, an integral part of your vision. You can't embark on a meaningful journey without first knowing your destination, without having a clear understanding of where you're headed. Your destination is your resting place, the sanctuary where you find solace and fulfillment, the culmination of your efforts, the embodiment of your dreams.

Do not, under any circumstance, leave this earth without pursuing your vision, without striving to realize the dreams that reside within your heart. To do so is a premature departure, a symbolic gesture of a life unlived, a wasted opportunity, a life devoid of its intended purpose. It's to leave behind a legacy of regret, a testament to untapped potential, a symphony left unfinished.

Just as the activities of a physical journey are carefully planned and executed with the destination in mind, your life's activities—your choices, your actions—should be guided by your vision. Your vision should serve as the compass that directs your course, the blueprint that shapes your decisions, the driving force that propels you forward. Vision is the distinguishing factor that separates leaders from followers, pioneers from imitators, creators from consumers. It's the ability to see beyond the present, to envision a future that's both desirable and attainable, and to inspire others to join you on the journey.

While we may all harbor desires and hopes, fleeting glimpses of a better future, without the anchoring force of vision, our lives remain unfocused, our efforts scattered, and our impact diminished. We become like leaves adrift in the wind, tossed about by the currents of circumstance, unable to find a stable footing, unable to leave a lasting mark. Vision provides the anchor, the stability, the focus that enables us to navigate the complexities of life and to achieve our full potential.

Vision is the starting point, the genesis of purpose, the architect of fulfillment. It's the understanding that we're not merely passive recipients of fate, but active creators of our own destinies. It's the realization that we have the power to shape our lives, to leave a positive impact on the world, and to create a legacy that transcends our own existence. It's the unwavering belief in the possibility of a better future, and the unwavering commitment to making that future a reality.

Vision: Connecting the Present to the Future

Understanding your vision propels you to action, transforming aspirations into tangible realities. Your vision provides direction, shaping your future goals and guiding you toward meaningful achievements. However, while aspirations are rooted in vision, our present is often shaped by immediate desires—our needs and wants—that demand attention.

Where there is a need, there is a desire. Needs are essential for survival and well-being, such as food, shelter, and security. Wants, on the other hand, are personal preferences or luxuries that enhance life, like comfort, status, or pleasure. Desire emerges from both, driving action in the present. Yet, focusing solely on immediate desires can lead to stagnation, trapping you in a cycle of routine and frustration.

Hope, in contrast, is forward-looking. It encompasses expectations and aspirations, shaping the future beyond immediate desires. Expectations are what we anticipate based on circumstances or effort, while aspirations are higher-level goals that align with our vision. Hope sustains motivation, bridging the gap between present desires and future fulfillment.

Until you bridge the gap between your now (needs and wants) and your future (hope), you risk living a frustrated, ordinary life—bound by anxiety and mundane routines, without time for yourself or your dreams. The key to transformation lies in intentional action: aligning present desires with future aspirations, ensuring that your vision not only inspires but also propels you toward a life of purpose and fulfillment. Vision serves as the crucial bridge connecting your present to your future. Without vision, desires can become misdirected, and hopes may prove to be in vain. Vision breathes life into both, transforming them into a powerful force for meaningful change. It ensures that desires are not merely fleeting impulses but purposeful steps toward a greater future.

Life is not solely about the present. The greater part of life is your future—the legacy you leave behind. How you manage your desires directly shapes that future. The most effective way to navigate desires is to anchor them in hope, allowing aspirations to guide your present decisions. A person of great hope is not consumed by immediate desires but instead focuses on long-term fulfillment. Let hope, not desire, dictate your life.

A person without vision lives for desire—for the "now," for immediate gratification. In contrast, a person with vision lives with the future in mind, practicing delayed gratification, understanding that destiny holds greater significance than momentary needs. Not every need is a necessity. Vision grants the courage to look beyond the present and hold onto future hopes. Hope never disappoints. Where there is hope, there is a willingness to wait patiently, and patience is always rewarded.

Vision fosters expectation, cultivating anticipation and excitement for what lies ahead. Those who are expectant are hopeful, and hopeful individuals are disciplined—full of restraint and resolve. With vision, hope becomes more than a distant wish; it transforms into a guiding force, shaping a life of purpose, patience, and fulfillment.

> As Romans 8:24-25 states, ***"But hope that is seen is no hope at all. Who hopes for what they already have? But if we hope for what we do not yet have, we wait for it patiently."***

This highlights how true hope looks beyond the immediate, empowering us to wait with discipline for the future we envision.

Vision and Leadership

Effective leadership is all about vision. It goes beyond just managing the here and now, instead focusing on connecting our present with a better future. This means tackling today's issues while also setting things up for a brighter tomorrow. This crucial ability to connect the **"now"** with the **"what could be,"** transforming aspirations into tangible realities, is solely empowered by vision. Without it, leadership risks becoming a hollow exercise in administration, lacking the transformative power to inspire and elevate.

Vision acts as a powerful catalyst, rekindling dormant desires, igniting imagination, infusing hearts with hope, and strengthening faith. It is the spark of progress, the fuel propelling us toward our goals. Until you truly grasp your vision, until you clearly see your desired destination, your life risks remaining confined within the ordinary, unable to grow or expand beyond familiar limitations, and falling short of its full potential.

Growth, in all its forms, is the reward of those who dare to venture beyond comfort, stepping outside the ordinary to embrace the challenges of the unknown. It belongs to those who stretch their faith, expand their minds, and believe in the extraordinary potential within them. We are not called to a life of mediocrity—a mundane existence devoid of purpose and passion—but to an extraordinary life where possibilities abound, dreams materialize, and potential is fully realized. Vision is the architect of this tomorrow, the builder of bridges to that brighter future. It enables us to see beyond the present, to envision a better world, and to inspire others to join in making that vision a reality. It fosters the understanding that we are not passive observers but active shapers of our destinies.

A leader with vision possesses the ability to inspire, motivate, and empower others to achieve their full potential. They perceive future possibilities and communicate that vision with passion and conviction, creating a shared sense of purpose and a collective belief in the team's capacity for extraordinary results. Visionary leaders challenge the status quo, question conventional wisdom, and embrace innovation, understanding that progress necessitates change and willingly taking risks to achieve their goals, driven by a deep commitment to making a positive impact.

To live an extraordinary life and achieve the seemingly impossible, we must embrace the power of vision. We must dare to dream big, set ambitious goals, and believe in our capacity to achieve them. Cultivating a mindset of possibility—a belief that all things are achievable—and a commitment to action are essential to making our dreams a reality. The potential for greatness resides within each of us; it is our responsibility to cultivate it, embrace the power of vision, and live a truly extraordinary life. Let us dare to dream, believe, and achieve, building a future worthy of our inherent potential.

The Enduring Nature of Vision and Generational Impact

Achieving your vision is a journey, not a fixed endpoint. It calls for patience, persistence, and a willingness to adapt as circumstances change. You'll encounter setbacks and detours, but the key is to never lose sight of your ultimate goal. Realizing your vision offers the hope of a meaningful life—one filled with purpose and lasting impact, extending far beyond the present moment.

However long it takes, your vision will come to pass if you remain committed, if you stay true to your course. A vision's fulfillment may begin in your generation and conclude in the next, spanning the boundaries of time. But if you play your part, if you contribute your portion, you have lived a successful life, a life of lasting significance (See Hebrews 11:13, 39-40; 1 Chronicles 22:6-11).

The Chinese Proverb, "**One generation plants trees, another enjoys the shade,**" perfectly expresses the essence of generational impact. Your vision may not be fully realized in your lifetime, but your efforts will pave the way for future generations to reap the rewards. It is about building a legacy, creating a foundation upon which others can build and flourish.

If you abandon your vision, your time will pass, and you will lose out on the fulfillment of your destiny. Tragically, the vision, being beneficial to society, will then be fulfilled through someone else—

through another who dares to seize the opportunity. This represents a missed chance to contribute your unique gifts to the world.

Run with your vision, however big or small. Work at it with unwavering dedication, and it will bring fulfillment—a deep sense of satisfaction that comes from knowing you have made a difference. Don't worry about provision; the vision itself is meant to provide for you.

Provision Lies Within Vision: Unlocking Abundance

The profound truth underpinning the pursuit of vision is this: the very resources, opportunities, and unwavering support you need to bring your aspirations to life are not external; they are integral components of the vision itself. They reside within the seed of your dream, waiting to be unearthed, nurtured, and brought to life. When you wholeheartedly embrace your vision and commit to its realization, you unlock a realm of boundless possibilities, a flow of abundance that sustains your journey, empowers your actions, and ultimately leads you to your desired destination.

Your vision isn't merely a fleeting dream or a whimsical fancy that evaporates with the morning mist. It is a seed, a potent kernel of potential, containing within its core the blueprint for its own manifestation. It's a promise, a declaration of what is possible, a testament to human ingenuity and the boundless capacity for achievement. As you nurture this seed with your unwavering dedication, diligent effort, and steadfast faith, it will blossom into a vibrant reality, a tangible manifestation of your dreams that surpasses even your most optimistic expectations.

Imagine a seed planted in fertile soil. It holds within its shell the potential for a mighty tree—a source of sustenance, shelter, and beauty. However, the seed alone can't bring this potential to life; it requires the nurturing elements of sunlight, water, and fertile ground. Similarly, your vision needs the nurturing elements of your dedication, your effort, and your unwavering belief.

The resources you need, the opportunities that arise, and the support you receive are all part of the ecosystem that surrounds your vision. They are the sunlight that nourishes your growth, the water that sustains your efforts, and the fertile ground that provides the foundation for your success.

When you embrace your vision, you activate this ecosystem. You attract the resources you need, recognize the opportunities that present themselves, and draw support from those who believe in your potential. It's as if the universe conspires to assist you, aligning circumstances and bringing together the elements necessary for your vision to flourish.

This isn't a magical process, but a natural consequence of your commitment. When you're clear about your vision and passionate about your goals, you radiate an energy that attracts positive influences. You become a magnet for opportunity, a beacon of hope for those who share your aspirations.

The abundance that flows from your vision isn't limited to material possessions or financial gain. It encompasses every aspect of your life, including your relationships, health, personal growth, and spiritual fulfillment. It is a holistic abundance, a sense of well-being that permeates your entire being.

To unlock this abundance, you must first cultivate a mindset of abundance. You must believe you are worthy of success, that you have the potential to achieve your dreams, and that the universe is a place of limitless possibilities. You must release any limiting beliefs or negative thought patterns that may be holding you back.

Then, you must take action. Nurture your vision with dedication and effort, seek out the resources you need, and seize the opportunities that arise. Be willing to overcome obstacles, learn from mistakes, and persevere through challenges.

As you embark on this journey, you'll discover that the power of your vision is far greater than you ever imagined. You'll witness the seed of your dream blossom into a magnificent reality, a testament to the power of human potential and the boundless abundance that resides within each of us. Your vision is not just a dream; it is a seed, a potential for growth and manifestation. As you nurture this seed with your dedication and effort, it will blossom into a reality that surpasses your expectations.

The Peril of Visionless Living

Never, under any circumstance, allow yourself to live without discovering your vision, without uncovering the unique purpose that resides within your soul. To exist without this guiding light is to live in perpetual uncertainty, profound disorientation, and a sea of confusion. It's to live a life devoid of its intended richness, falling short of its potential, and leaving behind a legacy of unfulfilled dreams and untapped possibilities.

Life, in its natural complexity, presents us with a wide variety of choices—a vast array of paths that diverge and converge, join and separate. Without vision, without a clear understanding of our purpose, we're susceptible to being swayed by external influences, led astray by fleeting trends, and trapped in cycles of unproductive activity. We become like a rudderless ship, tossed about by life's storms, unable to maintain a steady course or reach our desired port.

To live without discovering your vision is to live aimlessly, to wander without purpose, to drift without direction. It's to exist in perpetual motion yet make no real progress. It's to fill our days with activity yet find no true fulfillment, to accumulate experiences yet gain no lasting wisdom, and to chase after fleeting pleasures yet find no enduring happiness.

Vision, on the other hand, provides the clarity, focus, and direction that enable us to navigate life's complexities with purpose and intention.

It's the guiding star that illuminates our path, the compass that keeps us on course, and the fuel that propels us toward our goals. It's the understanding that our lives have meaning, that we have a unique contribution to make, and that we have the power to create a better future.

To discover your vision is to embark on a journey of self-discovery—a process of introspection and exploration that leads to a deeper understanding of your values, passions, and aspirations. It's to identify the unique talents and abilities you possess and to understand how you can use them to make a positive impact on the world.

It is to recognize that your life is not a random occurrence, but a purposeful creation, a masterpiece waiting to be unveiled. It is to understand that you have the power to shape your destiny, to create a life that reflects your values, and to leave a legacy that inspires others.

Therefore, never resign yourself to a life without vision. Seek out your purpose, explore your passions, and discover the unique contribution you are meant to make. Embrace the journey of self-discovery, and allow your vision to guide you toward a life of meaning, fulfillment, and lasting significance.

Vision is the root of inspiration and creativity, the catalyst that ignites your passion and fuels your drive. Grasp your vision, embrace its power, and you're on your way to living the success equation—a life of purpose, fulfillment, and lasting impact.

Self-Reflection and Vision

To really use the power of vision we've been talking about, it's good to spend some time thinking about yourself. Ask yourself these important questions. Let your answers help you see your path more clearly:

What do you picture for your life and where it's going? This first idea you have is like the very beginning of your vision. It's where your purpose and direction will come from.

What ideas do you have for your life? These little ideas are like the pieces you'll use to build your future. They're what you could do, just waiting for you to shape them.

What feeling do you have about where your life is headed? That gut feeling, that deep sense, often tells you what you're really capable of. It's like a quiet guide for your hopes.

What can you do about it? Just seeing what's possible isn't enough. This question makes you think about the actions you can take, the plans you can make, to get from where you are now to where you want to be.

What are you actually doing about it? This last question checks if you're really serious about your vision. It shows who just dreams and who actually makes things happen by taking steps forward.

When you really think about these things, your actions will have real meaning, you'll know why you're doing what you're doing, and you'll have a clear idea of where you're going. When you truly connect with the spirit of your vision, the one that comes from these thoughts, no problem will seem too big, and no challenge too scary. Because what you can see in your mind, you have the power to become in real life. Vision helps you rise above your current situation. You're meant to be led by what you see for yourself, not by what's happening around you right now, unless you decide to give up and believe that things can't be better. Regular people looked at the young boy David and just saw a shepherd. But vision saw a future king, someone who would lead a whole nation.

> ***"He chose David his servant and took him from the sheep pens; from tending the sheep he brought him to be the shepherd of his people Jacob, of Israel his inheritance." - Psalm 78:70-71***
>
> ***"So he told it to his father and his brothers; and his father***

> ***rebuked him and said to him, "What is this dream that you have dreamed? Shall your mother and I and your brothers indeed come to bow down to the earth before you?"... But his father kept the matter in mind." - Genesis 37:10-11***

The story of Joseph, who bravely shared his dreams of being important with his family, shows how powerful vision can be, even if people don't understand it at first. His brothers didn't believe him, and his father, Jacob, even told him off. But the Bible says Jacob **"kept the matter in mind."** This shows that even when a vision seems strange, it can still have a lasting impact. In the same way, God chose David, a simple shepherd, to be the leader of Israel. This teaches us that vision can see what someone can become, even if they don't seem special at the moment. His simple beginnings didn't stop him from becoming great, because a bigger vision saw his potential. So, take time to think about yourself, pay attention to the visions that come to you, and take action with confidence to make that amazing future a reality.

Cultivating Vision: Practical Steps

Reflection and Introspection:

Set aside quiet time for reflection and introspection.

Ask yourself:

- What am I passionate about?
- What are my unique talents and abilities?
- What impact do I want to make on the world?

Journal your thoughts and ideas, allowing your vision to emerge from the depths of your being.

Visualization and Imagination:

- Create a mental picture of your preferred future.
- Visualize yourself achieving your goals, living your dreams, and making a difference in the world.

Use your imagination to explore possibilities and create a compelling vision of your destiny.

Seeking Divine Guidance:

- Pray for wisdom and guidance, asking God to reveal your purpose and vision.
- Study the scriptures, seeking inspiration and insight from the lives of those who have followed their divine calling.
- Listen to the still, small voice within, the voice of intuition and divine guidance.

Writing and Articulating Your Vision:

Write down your vision in clear and concise terms.

- Create a vision board, a visual representation of your goals and aspirations.
- Articulate your vision to others, sharing your passion and inspiring them to join you on your journey.

Setting Goals and Creating Action Plans:

Break down your vision into smaller, more manageable goals.

- Create action plans, outlining the steps you need to take to achieve your goals.
- Set deadlines and hold yourself accountable for your progress.

Embracing Challenges and Overcoming Obstacles:

View challenges as opportunities for growth and learning.

- Develop resilience and perseverance, refusing to give up on your vision.
- Seek support from mentors, coaches, and trusted advisors.
- Living Your Vision Every Day:
- Align your daily actions with your vision.
- Make choices that support your goals and aspirations.
- Celebrate your progress and acknowledge your achievements.

The Legacy of Vision

Vision is not merely a personal pursuit; it is a legacy, a gift that you leave for future generations. By embracing your vision, you contribute to the ongoing story of humanity, leaving a lasting mark on the world.

Remember, your vision is not just a dream; it is a calling, a divine mandate to fulfill your purpose and make a difference. Embrace your vision, and you will unlock the extraordinary life that awaits you.

III

PART C: The Indispensable Foundation of Self-Preparation

There is no preparation more vital than self-preparation. To assert that it is the paramount prerequisite for success is not an exaggeration. Indeed, it is far better to be prepared for an opportunity that does not materialize than to encounter an opportunity for which you are unprepared.

4

KNOWLEDGE: THE FOUNDATION OF ACHIEVEMENT

"The heart of the discerning acquires knowledge; the ears of the wise seek it out." - Proverbs 18:15

"Every prudent man acts out of knowledge, but a fool exposes his folly." - Proverbs 13:16

"It is not good to have zeal without knowledge, nor to be hasty and miss the way." - Proverbs 19:2

"By wisdom a house is built, and through understanding it is established; through knowledge its rooms are filled with rare and beautiful treasures. A wise man has great power, and a man of knowledge increases strength." - Proverbs 24:3-5

There is no preparation more vital than self-preparation—the deliberate pursuit of knowledge, skill, and wisdom. To claim it as the paramount prerequisite for success is no exaggeration. For as Scripture warns, **"zeal without knowledge"** leads to ruin, while **"the prudent act with understanding."**

The parable of the ten virgins (Matthew 25:1-10) highlights this truth. Five were wise, bringing extra oil for their lamps; five were foolish, unprepared when the bridegroom arrived. The moment of opportunity revealed their readiness—or lack thereof. So it is in life: preparation determines possession.

Consider the athlete who wins gold in seconds, the coach who lifts the World Cup, the scholar who aces an exam—each achievement is the fruit of relentless preparation. Success is not seized in an instant; it is claimed by those who have already done the work.

The Principles of Self-Preparation

1. *Readiness is a Choice – You are never truly ready until you prepare.*

2. *Preparation Earns Favor – It draws recognition and opens doors.*

3. *There Are No Shortcuts – Neglect leads to missed opportunities; diligence leads to mastery.*

4. *Unprepared Visions Die – Many dreams fail for lack of disciplined groundwork.*

5. *Self-Achievement Demands Self-Preparation – There is no other reliable path.*

6. Preparation is Power – It equips you to overcome life's greatest challenges.

> As Happy Mulwe wisely said, ***"You prepare by packaging yourself appropriately."***

This means cultivating knowledge, sharpening skills, and fortifying mindset—continuously. For in the end, preparation is the only certainty in an uncertain world, ensuring that when opportunity knocks, you are not just present—you are ready.

The Twofold Power of Knowledge: Instruction and Information

Knowledge plays two vital, interconnected roles in our lives. To truly grasp its transforming power, we can think of it as both **"in-struction"** (building our inner structure) and **"in-formation"** (shaping our inner being). This distinction emphasizes that both practical guidance and a deeper inner understanding are essential for a life filled with purpose and fulfillment.

In-Struction: Building Your Life's Framework

Knowledge as "in-struction" provides the foundational structure for our lives. It's like the master blueprint for your inner world, giving you the essential principles and values that guide your decisions and actions. This aspect of knowledge acts as a roadmap, helping you navigate life's complexities, keeping you on your intended path, and avoiding potential pitfalls. Ultimately, **"instruction"** is about the practical application of knowledge—equipping you with the tools, techniques, and wisdom necessary to build a meaningful and successful life. When knowledge is actively applied, it transforms from mere understanding into a powerful force for growth, direction, and achievement.

As Proverbs 24:3 states, **"Through wisdom a house is built..."** This **"wisdom"** is your inner structure—the clear **"how-to"** that builds the solid framework of your life. It's like having a smart builder who knows exactly how to put things together so your life stands strong, forming the fundamental bones of your inner self.

In-Formation: Shaping Your Inner Being

In contrast, knowledge as "in-formation" focuses on your inner transformation. It molds and shapes you from within, aligning your character and actions with your inherent purpose. This is an internal process where knowledge shapes your beliefs, values, and worldview, ultimately guiding you toward your destiny and the realization of your full potential. **"Information"** delves into the **"why"** behind your actions, fostering a deeper understanding of your purpose and the meaning that drives you, thus creating profound inner change.

Proverbs 24:3 continues, **"And by understanding it is established..."** This **"understanding"** is the deep **"in-formation"** that firmly establishes your inner house. It's the inner process where you truly get why certain principles are important, allowing them to settle deeply into your character, making your inner self stable and unshakable.

The Divine Architect and Your Role

Knowledge, encompassing both instruction and information, is crucial for personal growth and achievement. Just as a building is carefully constructed according to its intended design, our lives should be structured and formed in alignment with our divine purpose. We aren't passive observers in life but active instruments of destiny, each designed to fulfill a specific role.

Consider the analogy of an architect who creates a design and a construction engineer who brings that vision to life. The engineer must adhere to the architect's design. The architect, in this analogy, represents the divine source or higher purpose that has a blueprint for your life, as suggested by Jeremiah 29:11—a plan for well-being, hope, and a positive future. This design isn't a rigid, predetermined path, but a framework of potential and purpose.

You are the construction engineer. You take this divine design and translate it into reality, actively wielding the **"tools and materials"**—your talents, abilities, opportunities, resources, and, crucially, your knowledge.

The critical point is your responsibility to follow the divine design. If an engineer deviates significantly from the plans, using poor materials or ignoring structural guidelines, the building will be flawed and unstable. Similarly, if we, as the **"engineers"** of our own lives, disregard the underlying principles and guidance (the "divine design"), we risk building a life that's less fulfilling, less purposeful, and potentially riddled with **"faults"** or **"structural weaknesses"**—perhaps in our character, our relationships, our careers, or our overall well-being.

Your pursuit of knowledge, both as instruction and information, is key to becoming a skilled and effective "engineer."

"Instruction" provides the **"how-to"**—the techniques, best practices, and fundamental principles needed for sound construction. This means learning skills, gaining practical wisdom, understanding ethical frameworks, and developing effective habits. Without this instruction, your efforts might be misdirected, inefficient, or even harmful, leading to a poorly constructed life.

"Information" gives you a deeper understanding of the **"why"**

behind the design, helping you grasp the architect's purpose and intention. This involves self-reflection, understanding your values, connecting with your inner purpose, and gaining wisdom about the world and your place in it. Without this deeper "information," you might build diligently but without a clear understanding of the ultimate goal, potentially constructing something that doesn't truly align with your deeper needs and aspirations.

Filling Your Life with Riches

The quality and outcome of your life's construction are directly influenced by your commitment to acquiring and applying knowledge. The more you understand the **"design"** (through introspection and spiritual guidance) and the more proficient you become in the **"engineering"** (through learning and practical application), the more likely you are to build a life that is strong, purposeful, and aligned with its intended potential—a life that embodies the prosperity, hope, and future envisioned. You're not just a random builder; you have a design to work from, and the knowledge you gain empowers you to bring that design to magnificent fruition.

> Proverbs 24:4 concludes, ***"By knowledge the rooms are filled with all precious and pleasant riches."***

This "knowledge" is the "in-formation" that fills every "room" of your life. Once your life's foundation is solid, this knowledge makes every part of it vibrant and full. It's like furnishing each room with beautiful and valuable things—not just stuff, but rich experiences, meaningful connections, inner peace, and a deep sense of purpose. This knowledge truly shapes and completes your inner self, making your life a treasure.

Without practical "in-struction," achieving anything of lasting value becomes impossible. Conversely, without deeper "in-formation," understanding remains elusive, leading to confusion and distraction. To accomplish anything meaningful, to realize our potential, and to leave a lasting legacy, we must diligently seek both. Therefore, acquiring knowledge stands as the initial and most vital step toward realizing our vision and fulfilling our destiny.

Knowledge as Illumination

Knowledge is the divine light that illuminates God's abundant provision, revealing the clear path to a life of prosperity and fulfillment. Picture the very beginning: God's first act was to create light, pushing back the deep darkness that covered the formless void. Without knowledge, our lives can feel much like that dark, empty space—lacking direction, shape, and true purpose.

> As Genesis 1:2-3 vividly describes, ***"Now the earth was formless and empty, darkness was over the surface of the deep... And God said, 'Let there be light,' and there was light."***

Just as God began with light, we too must begin by equipping ourselves with knowledge. This isn't just about collecting facts; it's about embracing both "in-struction" (the practical guidance that builds our inner strength) and "in-formation" (the deeper understanding that shapes who we are from the inside out). This dual nature of knowledge should hold the highest place in our lives, acting as a constant light that clarifies our vision and calling. It achieves this by renewing our minds, transforming how we see the world, and vastly expanding our understanding. A mind left in darkness, clinging to old ways, leads to a stagnant life—one without growth, progress, or genuine vibrancy.

Life, by its very nature, is dynamic, a constant flow of change and evolution. At its heart lies creativity, the driving force behind all innovation and advancement. Without creativity, life becomes dull, monotonous, and unfulfilling. But to truly be creative, we need a mind that is continually renewed—a mind open to fresh ideas, diverse perspectives, and boundless possibilities. This renewal of the mind is the key to true transformation. It's the process by which we break free from the limiting beliefs and patterns of our past, enabling us to fully embrace the incredible potential of our future.

> This profound truth resonates through scripture, as Romans 12:2 urges us, ***"Be transformed by the renewing of your minds,"*** and Ephesians 4:23 reminds us to ***"be renewed in the spirit of your mind."***

It's an active, ongoing process of letting God's truth reshape our thoughts, attitudes, and ultimately, our entire being.

The Mind as the Control Tower

New exploits, new achievements, and new levels of success are the demands of a dynamic life. To meet these, a transformed mind—one willing to embrace change and explore new horizons—is essential. The proverb "**You cannot teach an old dog new tricks**" aptly highlights the importance of adaptability and the ability to learn in this pursuit.

> This concept is further illustrated by the wisdom in Matthew 9:16-17: ***"No one sews a patch of unshrunk cloth on an old garment, for the patch will pull away from the garment, making the tear worse. Neither do people pour new wine into old wineskins. If they do, the skins will burst, the wine will run out,***

> ***and the wineskins will be ruined. No, they pour new wine into new wineskins, and both are preserved."*** This analogy makes it clear: new growth requires a new foundation.

Indeed, a winning journey starts with the right mindset. Consequently, the greatest battles are truly won within the mind, establishing the bedrock for all success. This highlights the understanding that external victories are often mere reflections of internal triumphs, and that the battleground of the mind is where true and lasting victories are forged. Just as you cannot pour new wine into old wineskins, you cannot reach new heights with old habits, old patterns of thinking, and old limitations. Transformation necessitates a renewed mind, one that is aligned with your vision and empowered by knowledge.

Knowledge, therefore, plays a pivotal role in this transformation. It shapes our attitude, which in turn determines our altitude—our level of success. You cannot soar beyond the boundaries of your knowledge; it defines your realm of possibility and the scope of your achievements. The more knowledge you acquire, the greater your potential and the wider your horizons become.

Think of the mind as the control tower, the command center that directs your actions and shapes your reality. What controls your mind ultimately controls you. Our existence is largely sustained by feeding the mind with knowledge, nourishing it with information, and empowering it with understanding. In essence, a person's life is known by their mind—their thoughts, their beliefs, and their perspectives. Your position and adequacy in life directly depends on the state of your mind—its clarity, its focus, and its resilience. The power to elevate your life lies in acquiring knowledge, in expanding your mental horizons, and in transforming your thinking. Knowledge is your key to freedom and your passport to success. Your current state and circumstances are a direct product of your current knowledge, beliefs, and actions, a truth echoed in Proverbs 23:7: "**For as he thinks in his heart, so is he.**"

Ultimately, you are shaped by your thoughts, molded by your beliefs, and defined by your perspectives. External forces cannot fundamentally change you without influencing your mind, altering your thoughts, and transforming your beliefs. Remember, your thoughts become words, your words become actions, your actions become habits, and your habits become character. With the right knowledge, instruction, and information, you possess the potential to become who you believe you can be and to achieve what you believe you can achieve. Therefore, until you change your thinking, until you transform your mind, you cannot change your position, you cannot alter your circumstances, and you cannot truly fulfill your destiny.

The Danger of Ignorance and the Pursuit of Knowledge

Working without knowledge is like trying to find your way in complete darkness. Every step feels unsure, and you could easily stumble. This fundamental lack of understanding, or ignorance, is actually quite dangerous. It's akin to starving your mind, leaving it weak, unable to grow, and incapable of reaching its full potential. Just as a body without nourishment withers, a mind deprived of knowledge stagnates.

It's crucial to remember that being ignorant about something isn't a cause for shame—it's simply part of being human. We all start out not knowing vast amounts of things. However, choosing to remain in that state of ignorance, actively refusing to learn and understand, is where the true problem lies. This choice holds us back, preventing us from evolving. Life itself is a continuous process of learning; we're constantly growing our understanding of the world and ourselves. That's why seeking knowledge is a never-ending journey, a lifelong pursuit. You're never too old, too accomplished, or too "smart" to learn more; there's always new insight to gain and new perspectives to explore.

Think of knowledge as essential food for someone who's hungry—it's absolutely necessary for growth, for health, and even for simply functioning effectively in life. This deep desire to learn often comes from feeling the discomfort of ignorance itself—that gnawing sensation of not understanding, that powerful yearning to comprehend things better, to grow as a person, and to contribute something meaningful. When you truly feel that discomfort, when you acknowledge the gaps in your understanding, you realize that no effort is too great to gain knowledge. We acquire knowledge not by passive reception, but by actively learning, by truly striving to find information, process it, and make sense of it in a way that transforms our inner world. This active pursuit is the key to dispelling darkness and illuminating our path forward.

True learning isn't just about accumulating facts or going through life's motions; it genuinely emerges when you engage in thoughtful reflection on your experiences. It's the deliberate act of looking back, analyzing what happened, understanding why things unfolded, and identifying the lessons embedded within each moment—both successes and setbacks. This isn't passive observation; it's actively processing your interactions, challenges, and triumphs to extract meaningful insights.

Many argue that this ability to truly learn from living is the most essential human endeavor because it's what allows us to adapt, grow, and avoid repeating past mistakes. Consequently, the ability to learn effectively becomes one of the greatest skills you can cultivate. It's not just about absorbing information, but about making sense of it, connecting it to your existing understanding, and then applying those insights to shape a better future for yourself and those around you. This refined skill empowers you to continually evolve, making every experience a stepping stone to greater wisdom and capability.

Learning and living are profoundly inseparable—they're the two absolute fundamentals for genuine existence. Just as our physical life ceases the moment we stop breathing, our personal growth and vitality begin to diminish dramatically when we cease to learn. It's not necessarily a physical death, but a profound perishing of potential. Without continuous learning, our relevance in a rapidly changing world fades, our personal capabilities and potential shrink, and with them, the very opportunity for a dynamic, meaningful life diminishes. If you stop breathing, your body dies. If you cease actively engaging your mind and expanding your understanding, your intellectual and spiritual self, your capacity to thrive and contribute, effectively perishes. You become stagnant, unable to adapt, and disconnected from the evolving world around you.

Learning: A Pathway to Earning and Fulfillment

Moreover, learning is a direct, undeniable pathway to greater earning potential. This isn't just about financial income, though that's a significant part. The more skillfully and consistently you learn—whether through formal education, hands-on practical expertise, or even subtle personal development—the more value you inherently bring to any situation, organization, or relationship. This expanded knowledge strengthens your proficiency in any chosen field, making you more effective, innovative, and indispensable.

This creates a clear, almost unbreakable connection between what you learn and what you ultimately earn. This "earning" manifests in many forms: it could be tangible financial success, certainly, but also increased influence within your community or profession, greater respect from peers, and a much deeper sense of personal fulfillment that comes from mastering new challenges and contributing meaningfully. In a world that's constantly evolving, the ability to rapidly acquire and apply new knowledge keeps you not just relevant, but highly sought after, directly translating into greater opportunities and rewards in all aspects of your life.

Avenues of Learning

There are four primary avenues through which knowledge is acquired:

Reading:

Interpreting written words into information, transforming symbols into understanding. Reading stimulates creative thinking, expands your vocabulary, and broadens your perspectives. Read books by successful people, books that offer insights, knowledge, and wisdom. Books contain ideas, blueprints for success, and pathways to achievement. Reading gives you access to counsel, guidance, and mentorship from those who have walked the path before you.

Note: The Bible is the ultimate book, the foundation of wisdom, the source of truth, and the guide to life. Every success principle, every ethical value, and every moral compass is rooted in its teachings.

Study:

> ***"Study to show yourself approved unto God, a workman that needs not to be ashamed, rightly dividing the word of truth"*** - 2 ***Timothy*** 2:15.

Go beyond reading, delving deeper into the subject matter, searching for answers, and seeking understanding. Study is investigative reading, a process of discovery and recovery, a journey into the depths of knowledge.

> ***"It is the glory of God to conceal a matter; but the glory of kings is to search out a matter." - Proverbs 25:2.***

Study is not merely memorization; it is the process of connecting the dots, of building bridges of understanding, and of applying knowledge to practical situations.

Meditation:

Meditation, as outlined in Joshua 1:8 and Psalm 1:1-3, is not merely a passive exercise in contemplation; it is an active and focused mental engagement with the knowledge you have acquired. It follows study, acting as a bridge between information and understanding. It is not about memorization, which is merely the retention of facts, but about transforming information into understanding for practical application, for real-world impact.

> ***"Understanding is a fountain of life to those who have it." - Proverbs 16:22.***

Understanding is the wellspring of wisdom, the source of clarity, and the foundation for effective decision-making. It empowers you to navigate complex situations, to solve intricate problems, and to make sound judgments.

> ***"And a man of understanding is of an excellent spirit." - Proverbs 17:27b.***

Understanding cultivates an excellent spirit, a spirit of discernment, wisdom, and resilience. It shapes your character, influencing your attitudes, your behaviors, and your interactions with others.

> ***"Then this Daniel was preferred above the presidents and princes, because an excellent spirit was in him." - Daniel 6:3.***

Daniel's exceptional spirit, cultivated through understanding and wisdom, distinguished him among his peers, elevating him to positions of influence and leadership.

> "***Good understanding wins favor." - Proverbs 13:15.***

Good understanding fosters favor, opening doors of opportunity and creating pathways to success. It enhances your ability to communicate effectively, to build strong relationships, and to navigate social dynamics.

Note: Meditation on God's Word is the cornerstone of understanding and wisdom. It is through the contemplation of scripture that we gain insight into God's character, His purpose, and His plan for our lives.

People: The Living Libraries of Knowledge

The fourth avenue of learning is through people, which will be explored in greater detail in Chapter 6. People are living libraries of knowledge, repositories of experience, and sources of wisdom. They offer diverse perspectives, unique insights, and valuable guidance.

Summary of Learning: A Lifelong Pursuit

Learning is a lifelong pursuit, an ongoing process of growth and development. It comes from two primary sources: books and people. Be present where knowledge is shared, actively engaging in learning opportunities, and seeking out mentors and advisors. Transform your attitude by renewing your mind, cultivating a mindset of curiosity, openness, and continuous improvement. Pursue formal education, attend seminars, read widely, and engage in meaningful conversations. The goal is not just having a vision, but achieving it, transforming aspirations into tangible realities. Vision is achieved through instruction and information, through the acquisition and application of knowledge.

The best way to leave this earth is to die empty, having fully utilized your potential, having shared your gifts, and having made a lasting impact. Acquire the knowledge to do so, to maximize your potential, and to fulfill your purpose. People perish from lack of vision and knowledge, from a failure to embrace the opportunities for growth and development.

> ***"My people are destroyed for lack of knowledge." - Hosea 4:6.***

Lack of knowledge leads to procrastination, which is the thief of time and opportunity, a subtle force that sabotages your progress and hinders your achievements. The sooner you empty yourself, the sooner you utilize your talents, the more fulfilled your life will be. Emptying requires skill, a refined ability to apply knowledge and execute tasks effectively.

> ***"If the axe is dull and its edge unsharpened, more strength is needed, but skill will bring success." - Ecclesiastes 10:10.***

Skill makes you a master, an expert in your field, a sought-after authority.

> ***"Do you see a man skilled in his work? He will serve before kings; he will not serve before obscure men." - Proverbs 22:29.***

Take responsibility to know your vision, to be informed and instructed, to equip yourself with the knowledge necessary to achieve your goals. Put on the armor of knowledge, preparing yourself for the challenges and opportunities that lie ahead. You are here on assignment, not to work by trial and error, but by purpose and design, to fulfill a specific role in God's plan. Be anxious to be fruitful, to maximize your potential, and to make a lasting impact. Think of it this way: your special talents are always there, they don't fade away. But your mind and body need constant attention to stay sharp. If you don't keep learning and growing, your mind can get a bit rusty, like a garden left untended where weeds take over. But if you keep learning and challenging yourself, your mind will blossom and produce amazing things!

> ***"I went past the field of the sluggard, past the vineyard of the man who lacks judgment; thorns had come up everywhere, the ground was covered with weeds, and the stone wall was in ruins." - Proverbs 24:30-31.***

You only live once. Equip yourself with knowledge, for **"in the grave, where you are going, there is neither working nor planning nor knowledge nor wisdom." - Ecclesiastes 9:10.**

Overcoming Obstacles to Knowledge Acquisition

Time Constraints:

Prioritize learning, allocating time for reading, study, and reflection.

Fear of the Unknown:

Embrace the unknown, viewing learning as an adventure, a journey of discovery.

Lack of Motivation:

- Find your passion, connecting learning to your goals and aspirations.

Information Overload:

- Focus on essential knowledge, filtering information, and prioritizing learning.

Negative Mindset:

- Cultivate a positive mindset, believing in your ability to learn and grow.

By overcoming these obstacles, you can unlock the transformative power of knowledge and create a life of purpose, fulfillment, and lasting impact.

The Power of Applied Knowledge

We are born with great curiosity, a thirst for understanding that propels us to explore the world around us, to absorb information, and to accumulate wisdom. Yet, the mere acquisition of knowledge, the accumulation of facts and figures, does not automatically translate into power, into the ability to effect change, or into the capacity to transform lives. Knowledge, in its raw, unapplied form, remains dormant, a potential force waiting to be unleashed.

It is the application of knowledge, the translation of abstract concepts into concrete actions, that brings true power, that creates tangible change, and that transforms lives in profound and lasting ways. Knowledge, like a seed, must be planted, nurtured, and cultivated to bear fruit. It is the act of applying knowledge, of putting it into practice, that allows us to reap the rewards of our intellectual pursuits.

Therefore, it is not enough to simply acquire knowledge, to fill our minds with information and insights. We must also actively apply it to our lives, to our work, and to our relationships. We must use our knowledge to solve problems, to create opportunities, to build stronger connections with others, and to make a positive impact on the world around us.

Imagine a skilled carpenter who possesses a vast knowledge of woodworking techniques. He can recite the properties of different types of wood, explain the intricacies of joinery, and describe the tools used in the craft. However, if he never picks up a hammer, if he never shapes a piece of wood, his knowledge remains theoretical, an untapped potential. It is only when he applies his knowledge, when he transforms raw materials into finished products, that his skill becomes evident, that his knowledge becomes power.

Similarly, a doctor who possesses a deep understanding of human anatomy and physiology, but who never treats a patient, never applies his knowledge to diagnose and heal, remains a student in theory. It is the application of his knowledge, the act of using his skills to alleviate suffering and restore health, that transforms him into a true physician.

Knowledge applied to our lives allows us to navigate the complexities of existence with greater wisdom and clarity. It empowers us to make informed decisions, to solve problems effectively, and to build a life that reflects our values and aspirations. It allows us to learn from our experiences, to grow from our mistakes, and to continuously improve ourselves.

Knowledge applied to our work enables us to excel in our chosen fields, to innovate and create, and to contribute to the progress of society. It allows us to develop new skills, to overcome challenges, and to achieve our professional goals.

Knowledge applied to our relationships strengthens our connections with others, fosters empathy and understanding, and builds bridges of communication. It allows us to resolve conflicts, to support and encourage others, and to create a harmonious and fulfilling social environment.

The power of applied knowledge lies in its ability to transform not only our own lives, but also the lives of those around us. It is the catalyst for positive change, the force that drives innovation, and the foundation upon which a better future is built. Therefore, let us not merely be collectors of knowledge, but active practitioners, transforming our understanding into action, and our potential into reality. Let us use our knowledge to build a world that is more just, more compassionate, and more fulfilling for all.

5

THE ENGINE OF POSSIBILITY

"Everything is possible for him who believes." - Mark 9:23

You are made of what you believe, and you can only live according to your vision if you believe.

The Tragedy of Unbelief

The true tragedy of human potential lies in the profound disconnect between knowledge and belief. Many people encounter powerful knowledge about their inherent abilities, their divine purpose, and their vast capacity for greatness. Yet, despite hearing or reading these truths, they fail to truly believe them deep within their hearts. Consequently, they languish in mediocrity, trapped in cycles of poverty and failure, simply unable to break free from the self-imposed limitations of their own minds. As Hebrews 4:2 (author's paraphrase) reveals,

> ***"But the message they heard was of no value to them, because those who heard it did not believe it."***

Faith is the tangible fruit of believing—the outward manifestation of an inward conviction. Faith isn't a passive thought; it's action, a dynamic force that moves in direct accordance with your deepest beliefs. How and what you believe fundamentally shapes your faith, determining the direction, intensity, and effectiveness of your actions. Faith is the living expression of your beliefs, the embodiment of your convictions. Conversely, wrong or wavering beliefs lead to a lack of genuine faith, resulting in a double-minded, unfruitful life characterized by inconsistency and stagnation. As Hebrews 11:6 powerfully states,

> ***"But he who comes to God must believe that He is a rewarder of those who diligently seek Him."***

This highlights that belief isn't just a mental assent, but a foundational conviction that drives courageous pursuit and expectation of reward.

Belief: The Catalyst for Transformation

Knowledge is indeed power, but its true strength and foundation lie in belief. In its raw form, knowledge is static—a potential that remains dormant until ignited by the spark of belief. The effectiveness of knowledge, therefore, is directly proportional to the degree to which you believe it. You can only believe within the realm of your knowledge, within the boundaries of what you understand to be true. Ultimately, belief gives life to knowledge, transforming it from a passive collection of facts into an active force for change.

Beyond mere activation, belief also gives knowledge practical value. It transforms knowledge from a theoretical concept into a practical tool for success. Anything of true value raises your standard of living, enhancing your quality of life and expanding your horizons. This empowering aspect of belief is evident in the determination it fosters:

you find the resolve to overcome obstacles and persevere through challenges when you genuinely believe in your ability to succeed. Belief fuels the determination to rise after a fall, to learn from setbacks, and to emerge stronger and more resilient.

Furthermore, belief empowers you to persevere even when you are alone, facing adversity without external support. When you truly believe, you are not frustrated by a lack of external validation; your vision remains steadfast even when the world does not applaud or others fail to recognize your potential. This unwavering resolve stems from a higher purpose. Believers are God-pleasers, not world-pleasers, driven by a divine calling and motivated by a greater mission. They are remarkably focused on their goals, determined to endure to the end and complete the task set before them. As Hebrews 12:2 states,

> ***"Looking unto Jesus the author and finisher of our faith; who for the joy that was set before him endured the cross, despising the shame, and is set down at the right hand of the throne of God."***

No matter how difficult life has been or how many setbacks you have experienced, your inherent value and potential remain undiminished if you believe. You are not a loser if you maintain faith in your ability to make a difference and contribute to the world. Indeed, you are not a victim of circumstance, but a victor in Christ, empowered to overcome any challenge. As 2 Peter 1:3 assures us,

> ***"His divine power has given us everything we need for a godly life through our knowledge of him who called us by his own glory and goodness."***

Embracing the Power of the Present Moment

Stop believing that your time to prosper, your time to succeed, is relegated to some distant future. Instead, believe that today is your day, that this very moment is your opportunity. As the powerful declaration states, **"Let the weak say, 'I am strong'; let the poor say, 'I am rich'; let the bound say, 'I am free'; and let the sick say, 'I am healed' because of what the Lord has done for us."** This is a call to align your present confession with God's ultimate provision.

Rise to the Challenge with Unwavering Faith

Rise up and do something challenging today—something that stretches your abilities, something that pushes you beyond your comfort zone. Do it with unwavering belief, knowing that, as Philippians 4:13 declares, **"I can do all this through him who gives me strength."** This isn't just a motivational phrase; it's a profound truth that empowers you to tackle any obstacle.

Engineered for Success: Your Divine Heritage

You are an overcomer, a conqueror, a victor. God's report is clear: no situation, no circumstance, no challenge can ultimately overcome you. Believe it! Maintain a cheerful spirit and a positive attitude, and every storm will calm down, every obstacle will be overcome. There is nothing impossible concerning your success, no limit to your potential. Success is not merely a possibility; it is your birthright, your divine inheritance. This means it's not something you have to earn from scratch or a privilege reserved for a select few. Rather, it's a right woven into the very fabric of your being, intended for you by design from the beginning. However, this profound promise is accessed only through belief, through unwavering faith. It's not a passive inheritance, but one that requires your active internal agreement and conviction.

This highlights that success is not accidental; it is your portion, your designated path. You weren't created for struggle or perpetual defeat. Instead, you are engineered for success, designed to thrive, and destined to flourish. This isn't just wishful thinking; it speaks to the inherent capabilities and potential placed within you. It's your heritage, your legacy, your divine inheritance—a predetermined outcome that awaits your activation. Conversely, failure is the accident, the deviation from your intended course. It's not your permanent state or ultimate destiny, but a temporary misstep, a detour that can be corrected when you realign with your true design.

> As Isaiah 54:17 (author's paraphrase) powerfully confirms: ***"No weapon forged against you will prevail, and you will refute every tongue that accuses you. This is the heritage of the servants of the Lord."***

This promise directly supports the idea that you are fundamentally designed for victory. It reassures you that external opposition cannot ultimately defeat you, and that you possess the inner strength to overcome criticism, doubt, and every challenge. This divine assurance highlights your inherent strength and protection on your path to fulfilling your victorious purpose.

The Power of Belief and Confession

What you hold to be true—the bedrock of your personal philosophy—ultimately determines your actions, the nature of your interactions, and the very essence of who you become. Your beliefs are the silent architects of your destiny, the unseen forces that guide your choices and influence your outcomes.

Belief serves as the vital catalyst that perfects your confession, aligning your spoken words with the deepest desires of your heart. This alignment empowers your speech with the undeniable force of truth. When your words resonate with the unwavering certainty of your beliefs, they become more than mere utterances; they transform into powerful declarations, affirmations of your inner convictions, and blueprints for your future. The words you choose and the declarations you make have the potential to shape your opportunities, mold your reality, and influence the very trajectory of your destiny.

> The ancient wisdom of Proverbs 18:21 reminds us that ***"the tongue has the power of life and death..."***

This profound statement highlights the immense power inherent in our words—their ability to create or destroy, to build up or tear down, to inspire or discourage. Spoken with intention and conviction, words can fundamentally shape our perceptions, influence our emotions, and ultimately determine our actions.

However, this power isn't simply in the act of speaking. It's the quality of the words, the source from which they originate, that truly determines their impact. Words born from a heart filled with faith-inducing knowledge and infused with unwavering belief speak life and purpose. They create an atmosphere of possibility, a realm where dreams take root and aspirations blossom.

When your words are rooted in faith, when they're aligned with the truth residing within your soul, nothing can stand in your way. The power of your belief, amplified by the force of your confession, creates an unstoppable momentum that propels you towards your goals, overcoming any challenge that dares to impede your path.

The apostle Paul, in 2 Corinthians 4:13, echoes this sentiment, drawing upon the wisdom of the Psalmist:

> ***"It is written: 'I believed; therefore I have spoken.' With that same spirit of faith we also believe and therefore speak."***

This passage clearly highlights the profound interconnectedness of belief and confession—our words are a direct reflection of our inner convictions. When our faith is unwavering, our words become a powerful expression of that belief, a declaration of the reality we envision. We speak with confidence, conviction, and the certainty that our words will manifest in the world around us.

This isn't about wishful thinking or empty affirmations. It's about aligning our thoughts, beliefs, and words with the truth that resides within us—the understanding that we are created in the image of a powerful Creator and possess the capacity to shape our own realities.

By cultivating a mindset of belief, by nurturing our faith with knowledge and understanding, and by speaking words that reflect our inner convictions, we unlock the power to transform our lives and create a future aligned with our highest aspirations. We become architects of our own destinies, empowered by the transformative synergy of belief and confession.

Driving Out Double-Mindedness: The Key to Focus

Singleness of heart, an unwavering focus, is absolutely essential for success. To truly believe means agreeing with yourself—aligning your thoughts, your words, and your actions with your deepest convictions. This inner harmony is the bedrock of purposeful living.

Belief is a powerful force that actively drives out double-mindedness—that internal conflict which severely hinders focus, sabotages progress, and stifles achievement. As James 1:6-8 so clearly warns, "when you ask, you must believe and not doubt, because the one who doubts is like a wave of the sea, blown and tossed by the wind. That person should not expect to receive anything from the Lord; being double-minded and unstable in all they do." This vividly illustrates how a divided mind lacks conviction, leaving an individual unstable and unproductive, much like a wave without direction, ultimately preventing them from receiving what they seek. This internal conflict leaves you unpersuaded about your own destiny, making you vulnerable to doubt and susceptible to every distraction. Ephesians 4:14 further elaborates, stating that with firm belief,

> ***"we will no longer be infants, tossed back and forth by the waves, and blown here and there by every wind of teaching and by the cunning and craftiness of people in their deceitful scheming."***

Just as an infant lacks the stability to stand firm, a double-minded person is easily swayed by external influences and deceptive ideas, lacking the crucial inner anchor of conviction.

This brings us to a profound metaphor: **"It takes a live fish to swim upstream against the current. A dead fish is carried and tossed to and fro by the current."** This adage perfectly expresses the difference between a life guided by unwavering belief and one controlled by double-mindedness. The **"current"** represents the prevailing challenges, societal pressures, negative influences, and even internal doubts that can sweep you away from your true course. A **"dead fish"** symbolizes the double-minded individual, lacking internal vitality, purpose, and direction—passively carried by whatever forces come their way, never truly moving forward on their own terms. In stark contrast, a "live fish" embodies the person with unwavering belief—someone who possesses the inner strength, clarity of purpose, and fierce determination to actively navigate against the flow, choose their own path, and achieve their goals despite adversity. They are not victims of circumstance but active agents, steering their own lives with conviction and resilience.

Therefore, choose to be the live fish. Examine your heart today: where are you double-minded? Decide now to root out every doubt and fully embrace the singleness of heart that will propel you toward your destiny.

God Blesses Faith: The System of Success

God has designed a clear path to success, a bit like a well-thought-out project. It's a system of transformation that moves from an initial idea to a tangible outcome.

The System of Success

1. **Input**: Your Starting Point

This is where everything begins. Think of it as the raw materials or the potential you have. It includes your talents, fresh ideas, opportunities that come your way, or even challenges that can spark growth. This stage is full of promise, but it's still just potential, like a single seed waiting to be planted.

2. **Process**: Turning Potential into Reality

This is the heart of the system, where your raw potential gets shaped and developed. It takes diligent effort, honed skills, and a touch of innovation. You're actively working, learning, and finding clever ways to make things happen. This "process" is like the seed falling into the ground and "dying" in John 12:24—it's not a literal death, but a transformation where the seed breaks open to grow into something new. It's about investing your energy and taking the necessary steps to bring your vision to life.

3. **Output**: The Finished Result

Finally, the "output" is the tangible result of all your hard work. It's the finished product, the visible fruit of your labor, and the clear manifestation of what you envisioned. This is where your potential becomes a reality, like a single seed producing many.

Why God Blesses the Output

It's important to understand that God blesses the output—the actual work you produce, the visible results of your efforts. Thoughts and good intentions, while valuable as a starting point, are like barren seeds if they never lead to action. You can't expect a harvest if you don't plant anything.

This means you must sow to reap; you must act to achieve. Faith isn't just a passive belief; it's an active force that pushes you through the entire process. Just as a farmer shows faith in the soil by diligently planting and tending, we too must turn our beliefs into concrete actions. The blessing isn't for dormant potential, but for potential that's brought to life through dedicated and obedient effort. As John 12:24 reminds us,

> ***"Unless a kernel of wheat falls to the ground and dies, it remains only a single seed. But if it dies, it produces many seeds."***

This powerful verse shows us that true growth and abundance come when we bravely put our potential to work and allow it to transform.

Ultimately, God is indeed interested in the fruit—the tangible outcome—of our belief. He blesses the manifestation of faith through action, not just the intention.

The Visible Expression of Faith

Your work, regardless of its perceived size or significance, serves as a tangible expression of your faith. It reveals the depth of your convictions, the nature of your beliefs, and the extent of your knowledge. Faith is never static; it's a dynamic force that inherently leads to action. It's not enough to intellectually agree with a set of beliefs or to claim faith without demonstrating it in your daily life. Just as a tree is known by its fruit, your faith is revealed by your deeds. As James 2:18 proclaims,

> **"But someone will say, 'You have faith; I have deeds.' Show me your faith without deeds, and I will show you my faith by what I do."**

This verse powerfully reveals the inseparable link between faith and action. True faith isn't passive; it's active, dynamic, and transformative, compelling you to move and translate your beliefs into tangible results.

Consider it this way: your work, in all its forms, is the physical manifestation of your internal convictions. Whether it's the dedication you bring to your daily tasks, the integrity you display in your relationships, the compassion you show to others, or the pursuit of your greatest goals—these actions are not separate from your faith; they are a direct outgrowth of it. They provide a transparent window into what you truly believe, how deeply you're committed to those beliefs, and the understanding you possess. Every effort, every decision, every interaction becomes a testament to your inner world.

Faith without accompanying actions is described as "dead" because it lacks the very essence of life and purpose. As James 2:17 states, ***"In the same way, faith by itself, if it is not accompanied by action, is dead."***

It's like a magnificent blueprint for a building that is never constructed, or a seed that holds the potential for a vibrant plant but remains unplanted. The potential is undeniably there, but without the catalyst of action, it remains unrealized and ineffective. Your deeds are the breath that gives life to your faith, transforming it from an abstract concept into a living, impactful reality. They are the undeniable evidence that your beliefs are not just theoretical, but deeply ingrained and actively shaping who you are and what you do.

The Journey of Success: From Ear to Heart to Mouth

The journey towards achieving your potential and realizing success is deeply rooted in an internal process that unfolds in three key stages: from what you hear, to what you believe in your heart, and finally, to what you speak and do with your mouth. This progression highlights the profound impact of internal states on external outcomes.

The **"ear"** represents the reception of information, ideas, and influences from your environment. This is where the seeds of belief (or unbelief) are sown. What you consistently allow into your mind, through what you listen to, read, and engage with, directly shapes your internal landscape. This intake then travels to the **"heart,"** which the proverb identifies as "the wellspring of life" (see Proverbs 4:23). This isn't merely the physical organ, but rather the very core of your being – your mind, emotions, will, and conscience. It is the control center where convictions are formed, values are established, and faith takes root.

If this inner sanctuary, the heart, becomes corrupted by doubt, fear, negativity, or limiting beliefs, it's similar to polluting the source of a river. The contamination at the wellspring will inevitably affect everything downstream. A heart filled with negativity will produce negative thoughts, emotions, and ultimately, actions that sabotage progress. Doubt paralyses initiative, fear constricts potential, and negativity poisons motivation. When the heart is compromised, the entire system breaks down, hindering your ability to pursue goals, overcome challenges, and seize opportunities. Your efforts become half-hearted, your decisions clouded, and your potential remains untapped.

Therefore, guarding your heart is not a passive endeavor; it demands active, continuous vigilance. It's an intentional commitment to cultivating an inner environment conducive to success. This means:

Managing Your Input:

Be discerning about what you allow yourself to hear, watch, and consume. Seek out uplifting, empowering, and informative content. Surround yourself with positive influences and avoid those that foster doubt or negativity.

Cultivating Positive Thoughts:

Actively challenge negative thought patterns and replace them with constructive, hopeful ones. This is an ongoing mental discipline that strengthens your resilience.

Nurturing Healthy Beliefs:

Identify and uproot limiting beliefs that tell you what you can't do or achieve. Instead, cultivate beliefs in your own capabilities, in the potential for growth, and in the possibility of success. This involves affirming your strengths and focusing on solutions rather than problems.

Fostering Unwavering Faith:

This faith is not just in a higher power, but also faith in yourself, your abilities, and the process of growth. It's the conviction that despite obstacles, you can persevere and achieve your objectives. This kind of faith provides the internal strength and resolve needed to push forward.

Ultimately, what resides in your heart will inevitably find its way to your **"mouth"** – not just in the words you speak, but also in the actions you take. Your speech reflects your inner world, and your deeds are the outward manifestation of your deepest convictions. A heart brimming with faith and positivity will naturally produce words of encouragement, solutions, and purpose, leading to actions that propel you towards your goals. Conversely, a heart burdened by negativity will express itself in complaints, excuses, and inaction, hindering any real progress. The success you seek in the external world is a direct reflection of the inner work you commit to doing in your heart.

The Belief Cycle: Shaping Reality Through Knowledge, Faith, and Confession

The human experience is fundamentally driven by a powerful, continuous loop: the Belief Cycle. This dynamic interplay between knowledge, faith, and confession highlights the profound interconnectedness of our intellectual understanding, our emotional convictions, and our spoken declarations. It's through this continuous feedback loop that we actively shape our realities, mold our destinies, and ultimately manifest the life we envision.

Faith, the cornerstone of this cycle, isn't born from a vacuum. Instead, it emerges from hearing—from receiving and internalizing knowledge. Knowledge, in its raw form, is like a seed, a potent source of growth and transformation. Through the process of listening, absorbing, and processing information, this seed is planted in the fertile ground of our minds, setting the initial stage for belief to form.

With our heart, the seat of our emotions and convictions, we then believe, transforming mere knowledge into unwavering faith. We move beyond intellectual understanding to embrace a deeper, more profound conviction—a certainty that transcends mere logic and reason. This vital conversion of knowledge into belief is the catalyst that ignites the engine of our actions, preparing us for outward expression.

From the abundance of a heart overflowing with faith and conviction, the mouth speaks, confessing our beliefs and actively shaping our reality. Our words become the outward expression of our inner convictions, the tangible manifestation of our faith. They aren't just utterances, but powerful declarations—affirmations of the reality we envision, actively participating in its creation.

What you believe—the core tenets of your personal philosophy—ultimately determines your faith, the very foundation upon which you build your life. Your beliefs serve as the compass that guides your choices, the filter through which you interpret experiences, and the driving force propelling you towards your goals. How you believe, the manner in which you hold your convictions, in turn, determines your actions—the tangible expression of your faith. These actions, then, actively shape your reality, influencing your behaviors, outcomes, and future experiences.

The ancient adage, **"You are what you think,"** holds a profound truth here. Our thoughts, beliefs, and internal narratives shape our perceptions, influence our emotions, and ultimately dictate our actions. Thus, how you think—the patterns of your thought processes and the nature of your mental landscape—fundamentally shapes your reality, directly influencing your choices, behaviors, and outcomes.

This Belief Cycle isn't a static process; it's dynamic and ever-evolving. As we acquire new knowledge, our beliefs are challenged and refined. As our faith deepens, our confessions become more powerful and transformative. As our confessions shape our reality, our experiences reinforce our beliefs, creating a robust feedback loop that propels us towards our desired outcomes.

To harness the power of this cycle, we must be intentional about the knowledge we acquire, the beliefs we cultivate, and the confessions we make. We must actively seek out knowledge that aligns with our values and aspirations, cultivate beliefs that empower us to achieve our goals, and speak words that truly reflect our inner convictions. By consciously engaging in this continuous cycle of belief, we become the architects of our own destinies, empowered to shape our realities and create a life that reflects our highest aspirations. We transform our thoughts into actions, our beliefs into realities, and our dreams into tangible achievements.

Unleashing Your Inherent Greatness

The seed of greatness resides within your mind, a potent force capable of transforming your life and impacting the world. This isn't a mere abstract idea; it's an invitation to cultivate a vibrant landscape of creativity and achievement, to plant a forest of inventions and innovations. Your inherent greatness isn't confined by your circumstances, your past, or your current reality; it's simply waiting to be unleashed.

To truly tap into this potential, you must actively think and live outside your comfort zone. This means challenging your perceived limitations and continuously expanding your horizons. Don't passively think your living, existing within the confines of what's familiar and allowing routine to dictate your potential. Instead, dare to live your thinking, translating your boldest ideas into concrete action and embodying your beliefs in your daily life. This active engagement is the critical difference between stagnation and dynamic growth.

Crucially, don't let circumstances control your thinking. Allowing external factors—whether they be setbacks, opinions of others, or societal pressures—to dictate your mindset, attitudes, and behaviors is a common trap that severely limits your potential. Conversely, empower yourself by letting your thinking control your circumstances. This fundamental shift enables you to proactively shape your reality, overcome challenges, and create opportunities where none seemed to exist. This isn't just wishful thinking; it's living hopefully, maintaining a positive outlook and cultivating a steadfast belief in the tangible possibility of a better future.

Furthermore, don't be content with what you merely see—the immediate limitations of your physical senses or current situation. Instead, focus intently on what you think—the boundless potential of your mind. Remember, you are your thinking; your thoughts, beliefs, and perspectives define you and form the blueprint of your existence. Let this powerful internal landscape compel you to action, driving you to pursue your goals, overcome obstacles, and ultimately fulfill your destiny.

You are not inadequate, limited by your circumstances, or defined by your past. You are connected to an infinite source—a wellspring of power, wisdom, and creativity. You are a great person, endowed with unique talents, abilities, and limitless potential. Your greatness is boundless because you cannot out-think God, the ultimate source of all wisdom and knowledge. Therefore, believe in your potential, in your ability to achieve greatness, and in your capacity to make a lasting impact on the world. Embrace the transformative power of this belief, and you will unlock the extraordinary life that awaits you.

Belief is a powerful force, capable of transforming your life, your relationships, and your world. By embracing the power of belief, you can unlock your potential, achieve your dreams, and live a life of purpose, fulfillment, and lasting impact.

6

THE POWER OF SOCIAL INTERACTION

"He who walks with the wise grows wise." - Proverbs 13:20

"Those who do not interact will always be in* trouble.*" - Chibamba Kanyama

The Power of Connection: Thriving in Community

The human experience, at its most fundamental level, is defined by connection. We aren't solitary entities, self-sufficient islands adrift in a vast ocean of existence. By our very nature, we're social beings, deeply connected within a network of relationships, designed for connection and collaboration. Regardless of the brilliance of our minds, the depth of our talents, or the strength of our individual abilities, true and lasting success is rarely, if ever, achieved in isolation. We're created to thrive in community, to find strength in unity, and to experience the richness of shared endeavors.

This inherent need for connection is powerfully expressed in the concept of teamwork—the synergistic force that arises from the collective efforts of individuals working toward a common goal. It's clear that God, in His infinite wisdom, often works through people, through the intricate web of human connections, to propel us toward our destiny and guide us along the path of our purpose. We aren't meant to walk this journey alone; we're meant to journey together, to support one another, and to celebrate each other's successes.

The timeless wisdom of Ecclesiastes 4:9-12 beautifully illustrates the strength and resilience that come from connection:

> ***"Two are better than one, because they have a good return for their work: If one falls down, his friend can help him up. But pity the man who falls and has no one to help him up! Also, if two lie down together, they will keep themselves warm. But how can one keep warm alone? Though one may be overpowered, two can defend themselves. A cord of three strands is not quickly broken."***

This passage transcends the boundaries of time and culture, offering profound insight into the human need for connection. It emphasizes the critical importance of mutual support, the strength that arises from shared resources, and the collective power found in unity.

The image of a friend helping another who has fallen is a powerful representation of mutual support. Life's a journey filled with challenges, moments of doubt, and inevitable setbacks. We all stumble, we all fall, and we all experience difficult times. It is in these moments that the support of others becomes invaluable, providing the strength and encouragement we need to rise again and continue our path.

The analogy of two lying down together to keep warm highlights the power of shared resources and comfort. When we combine our efforts, our talents, and our resources, we can achieve far more than we could alone. We create a synergy, a collective force that amplifies our individual abilities and allows us to overcome obstacles that might be insurmountable on our own.

Finally, the image of a cord of three strands, not quickly broken, emphasizes the remarkable resilience and unwavering strength that come from unity. When we're deeply connected to others, we're stronger, more resilient, and better equipped to face life's challenges. We become part of something larger than ourselves—a community of individuals working together to achieve common goals. This interwoven strength provides an enduring foundation, making the collective far more robust than any individual thread.

This inherent need for connection isn't a weakness, but a profound strength. It's a recognition of our interdependence, our understanding that we're all part of a larger whole. It's also a commitment to building relationships based on mutual respect, trust, and unwavering support. By embracing the power of connection, we create a vital network that empowers us to achieve our goals, overcome challenges, and live a life of purpose and fulfillment. We become part of a thriving community, a network of individuals committed to helping each other succeed, ensuring we're not alone but connected, supported, and empowered to achieve our full potential.

The Influence of Association

The human journey is a continuous process of learning and character formation, a constant evolution shaped largely by the intricate network of social interactions that surround us. Our associations—the individuals we choose to engage with, the communities we become a part of—exert a profound and often subtle influence on our development, shaping our perspectives, influencing our decisions, and ultimately affecting the trajectory of our destiny. We're constantly receiving advice, counsel, and guidance, both consciously and unconsciously, from those with whom we interact, whether through direct conversation, shared experiences, or even the subtle cues of their behavior.

The ancient wisdom of Proverbs 27:17, **"As iron sharpens iron, so one person sharpens another,"** beautifully illustrates the power of constructive relationships to refine and improve us. Just as iron, through the friction of repeated contact, becomes sharper and more effective, so too do we grow and develop through interaction with others. The exchange of ideas, the sharing of experiences, and the mutual challenging of perspectives create a dynamic environment for personal growth.

Our circle of friends, the individuals we choose to confide in and share our dreams with, plays a crucial role in our well-being and success. Just as we exercise discernment in the books we read, carefully selecting those that enrich our minds and expand our understanding, so too should we be discerning about the individuals we allow into our inner circle. Our associations have the power to either elevate us, inspiring us to reach our full potential, or bring us down, hindering our progress and derailing our dreams.

Think of it like a garden. If you plant seeds of negativity, doubt, and skepticism, you'll inevitably reap a harvest of those same qualities. Conversely, if you plant seeds of positivity, encouragement, and ambition, you'll cultivate a garden of growth and achievement. The individuals we surround ourselves with become a reflection of our values, aspirations, and beliefs. They influence our thought patterns, shape our habits, and ultimately determine the direction of our lives. They can be our greatest cheerleaders, our most trusted advisors, and our unwavering sources of support. Or, they can be our harshest critics, most destructive influences, and greatest obstacles.

Therefore, it's essential to be intentional about the relationships we cultivate. Surround yourself with individuals who inspire you, who challenge you to grow, and who share your vision for the future. Seek out mentors who've achieved the success you aspire to, and learn from their experiences. Build relationships with individuals who are positive, supportive, and truly committed to personal growth.

Conversely, be mindful of relationships that drain your energy, diminish your confidence, and distract you from your goals. Distance yourself from individuals who are negative, skeptical, or who seek to undermine your aspirations. The influence of association is a powerful force that shapes our lives in profound and lasting ways. By carefully selecting our relationships and cultivating a network of positive, supportive individuals, we can create an environment that fosters growth, empowers us to achieve our goals, and ultimately leads us to a life of purpose and fulfillment. Remember, your journey is uniquely yours, and the people you choose to walk alongside you will have a significant impact on your destination. Choose wisely.

Evaluating Your Associations

The journey of life necessitates a periodic and honest evaluation of our associations—the individuals and communities that populate our social landscape. This isn't about judgment, but rather a crucial exercise in self-preservation and a deliberate act of ensuring our relationships align with our aspirations and support our personal growth. We must critically ask ourselves: Do these associations promote or hinder my vision? Do they serve as catalysts for my progress, or do they act as anchors, holding me back from achieving my full potential?

True friendships, the bonds that withstand the tests of time and circumstance, are characterized by a mutual commitment to growth and development. These relationships sharpen us mentally, challenging our assumptions, expanding our thinking, and encouraging us to step outside our comfort zones. They act as mirrors, reflecting our strengths and weaknesses, offering constructive criticism, and providing unwavering support. Worthy associations inspire a sense of responsibility towards our destiny, motivating us to pursue our goals with diligence and determination, to embrace challenges, and to persevere through setbacks.

The apostle Paul, in 1 Corinthians 15:33, issues a stark warning that highlights the deceptive and harmful nature of negative associations:

> ***"Do not be misled: Bad company corrupts good character."***

This timeless admonition highlights the subtle ways in which negative influences can erode our values, compromise our integrity, and ultimately derail our progress. Similarly, Proverbs 13:20 offers a cautionary tale:

> ***"He who walks with the wise grows wise, but a companion of fools suffers harm."***

This verse highlights the profound impact of our associations on our intellectual and moral development. Just as the company we keep can elevate us to new heights of wisdom, it can also drag us down into folly and ruin.

Since counsel, guidance, and influence inevitably flow from those with whom we spend our time, it's imperative that we choose our companions wisely. Wrong company inevitably brings wrong advice, leading us astray from our intended path and frustrating the fulfillment of our destiny. Proverbs 11:14 offers a sobering reminder:

> ***"For lack of guidance a nation falls, but many advisers make victory sure."***

This verse highlights the importance of seeking wise counsel and surrounding ourselves with individuals who possess the knowledge, experience, and wisdom to guide us on our journey. Proverbs 15:22

further reinforces this principle:

> ***"Without counsel, purposes are disappointed: but in the multitude of counsellors they are established."***

These proverbs highlight the value of diverse perspectives and the collective wisdom that arises from a multitude of counselors. By seeking out a variety of viewpoints, we can gain a more comprehensive understanding of our challenges and opportunities, and make more informed decisions.

Therefore, it's essential to actively cultivate a network of individuals who inspire you, challenge you, and genuinely support you on your journey. Seek out mentors who've achieved the success you aspire to, and learn from their experiences. Build relationships with individuals who are positive, supportive, and truly committed to personal growth. Conversely, be mindful of the relationships that drain your energy, diminish your confidence, and distract you from your goals. Distance yourself from individuals who are negative, cynical, or who seek to undermine your aspirations.

The evaluation of your associations isn't a one-time event, but an ongoing process. As you grow and evolve, your needs and aspirations will change, and your relationships should reflect those changes. Be willing to let go of relationships that no longer serve your highest good, and make room for new connections that will support your journey. Remember, your associations are a reflection of your values and aspirations, and they play a crucial role in shaping your destination. Choose wisely.

Beyond the Crowd: The Power of the "Involved"

The path to true success is not found in blindly following the crowd. Instead, it demands personal responsibility and self-accountability—a commitment to being true to yourself and laser-focused on your destiny. This journey requires discerning vigilance, particularly concerning the company you keep.

It's crucial to distinguish between mere acquaintances and those who are truly "involved" in your growth. The "involved" are individuals who actively support you, rather than exploiting you for their own gain. They're the ones who help confirm your purpose, offering essential affirmation and encouragement. When things seem hopeless, they motivate you to keep going, reminding you of your innate potential and inspiring you toward greater achievements. Furthermore, these valuable allies often serve as coaches and mentors, generously sharing their wisdom and experience to help you navigate the challenges on your path.

Unlike passive observers or those who would subtly undermine your efforts, the **"involved"** are actively invested in your success. They understand that a rising tide lifts all boats, and their support is a reflection of their own commitment to positive growth and shared success. Choosing to associate with such individuals means surrounding yourself with a network that uplifts, challenges constructively, and provides the guidance necessary to stay aligned with your purpose. This deliberate choice is a cornerstone of genuine progress and fulfillment.

These are the people you need in your life:

Those who confirm your purpose:

Like Mary and Elizabeth, who affirmed each other's calling (Luke 1:41-42, 45).

Those who help you see clearly:

Like Ananias, who restored Paul's sight and gave him direction (Acts

9:17).

Those who help usher you into your calling:

Like Barnabas, who championed Paul and introduced him to the apostles (see Acts 9:26–27).

Those who stay with you in hard times:

Like Ruth, who remained loyal to Naomi through hardship and loss (see Ruth 1:16–17).

Commitment, Purpose, and Divine Connection

The journey towards achieving our goals and realizing our vision is far from a solitary endeavor. God, in His desire for our success, strategically places individuals in our path—people who possess the capacity to support, encourage, and propel us towards our intended destination. However, the manifestation of these divine connections isn't a passive process. It hinges on our willingness to commit wholeheartedly to our purpose, to add tangible value to the lives of others, and to work diligently towards the realization of our goals.

Commitment, in its essence, acts as a powerful magnet, attracting the "involved" individuals whom God has blessed with the capacity to refresh and support us on our journey. It's a demonstration of our unwavering dedication, a testament to our resolve, and a clear signal that we are serious about our aspirations. When we commit to our purpose, we create an energetic field that draws like-minded individuals—those who resonate with our passion and share our vision.

Don't let anxieties about who will assist you distract you from your path. Trust your journey and stay focused on your goals, rather than worrying about external support. The right help often appears precisely when needed, a testament to divine timing. By actively pursuing your purpose with determination, you'll frequently find that people are surprisingly eager to assist you. It's your initiative and commitment, demonstrated through action, that truly invites the guidance and aid of others.

The attraction of the right people isn't predicated on outward appearances, superficial displays of wealth, or status. It's rooted in the intrinsic value of your purpose, the potential you possess, the gifts you've been given, and your unwavering commitment to making a positive difference in the world. It's about the substance of your character, the depth of your passion, and the clarity of your vision.

Therefore, dedicate yourself to the diligent development of your potential, to the cultivation of your skills, and to the clarification of your purpose. Invest in yourself, expand your knowledge, and refine your abilities. As you grow and evolve, as you become more aligned with your purpose, you will naturally attract the right people into your life—individuals who recognize your value and are eager to support your journey.

These individuals won't merely be passive observers; they will be active participants in your success, offering guidance, encouragement, and support. They will challenge you to grow, inspire you to reach higher, and celebrate your achievements alongside you. They will be your allies, your mentors, and your friends.

The process of attracting the right people isn't about manipulation or coercion; it's about authenticity and alignment. It's about being true to yourself, staying focused on your purpose, and radiating an energy that draws like-minded individuals into your sphere of influence.

Trust in the divine plan of your journey, knowing that God has placed the right people in your path. Focus on cultivating your potential, adding value to the lives of others, and working diligently towards your goals, and you will find that the right people will naturally gravitate towards you, eager to support you on your path to success.

Your Purpose in Serving Others

You aren't meant to be alone, isolated from the world. Instead, you're meant to be used fully, to contribute your unique talents and abilities, and your associations play a crucial role in helping you achieve this. Being a loner, disconnected from others, makes you less effective, limiting your impact and hindering your potential. This leads to a crucial reflection point: How is your attitude towards others?

Your success fundamentally depends on your willingness to serve and to add value to the lives of others. You are here to serve, to work, to contribute. Through work, you positively impact lives, creating an enabling environment for others to thrive. You reproduce yourself through work, leaving a legacy of impact and inspiration. Just as God has strategically ordained people to help you, you are meant to help others—to be a source of support, encouragement, and empowerment. We're meant to complement each other, not compete, recognizing the unique gifts and talents each individual brings to the table. You are here to do good to all, extending kindness and compassion to those around you. While you choose your friends, you don't get to choose whom to help, for you are God's servant, and all people are God's people, deserving of your compassion and assistance. You are a conduit of blessings, a channel through which God's love and grace can flow. While you cannot help everyone, you absolutely cannot afford not to help anyone.

> As Edward Everett Hale wisely noted: ***"If you can't do everything, it doesn't mean you can't do something. I am only one, but still I am one. I cannot do everything; but still I can do something. And because I cannot do everything, I will not refuse to do that something that I can do."***

This sentiment perfectly expresses our individual responsibility to act.

God's concern for your neighbor is precisely why you were born near them, why you are placed in your specific community. You are a solution to your environment, a catalyst for positive change. Your achievements don't just benefit you; they inspire others, motivating them to pursue their own dreams and reach their full potential.

Cooperation, Not Competition

God, in His infinite wisdom, never intended us to engage in a relentless battle for supremacy or a constant struggle to outdo one another. Instead, He designed us to complement each other, to recognize and celebrate the unique gifts and talents each individual brings to the table. We aren't meant to be clones or carbon copies; rather, we are diverse expressions of the divine, each possessing a unique purpose and a singular contribution to make.

No one can truly compete with you, for you are a unique creation, a singular expression of God's artistry. Similarly, you cannot truly compete with anyone else, for they too are unique, possessing their own distinct talents and abilities. We are all individuals, each with our own path to walk, our own role to play, and our own destiny to fulfill.

While we may have different paths, roles, and destinies, we are united in a common goal: to add value to the world, to make a positive impact on the lives of others, and to leave a legacy of contribution and compassion. No one can do what you were born to do—to fulfill the specific role God has designed for you. Your unique combination of talents, experiences, and perspectives makes you uniquely qualified to contribute to the world in a way no one else can.

> As the saying goes, ***"You are not meant to be better than your neighbor, but to be your best for your neighbor to be their best."***

This profound statement expresses the essence of true collaboration, the understanding that our own success is inextricably linked to the success of others. We aren't meant to strive for individual glory, but rather to work together, to support one another, and to create a world where everyone has the opportunity to thrive.

This understanding is powerfully reflected in the commandment: "Love your neighbor as you love yourself." This isn't merely a moral imperative; it's a fundamental principle of human flourishing. When we genuinely love our neighbors—when we treat them with respect, compassion, and empathy—we actively create a world of harmony and abundance. We build bridges of understanding, foster true collaboration, and unlock opportunities for everyone to succeed.

Competition, in its destructive form, breeds envy, resentment, and division. It creates a climate of fear and scarcity, pitting individuals against one another in a relentless pursuit of limited resources. Cooperation, on the other hand, fosters creativity, innovation, and abundance. It cultivates a climate of trust and collaboration, where individuals work together to achieve common goals and create a better world for all.

Let us embrace the spirit of cooperation, recognizing that our success is deeply intertwined with the success of others. Let us celebrate our differences, understanding that they are a source of strength and creativity. Let us work together, as partners in purpose, to build a world where everyone has the opportunity to thrive, to contribute, and to live a life of meaning and fulfillment. Let us be our best, so that our neighbors may be their best.

The Destructive Nature of Competition

While healthy competition is a vital component in the realm of business, fostering innovation and efficiency, it can become profoundly destructive in personal relationships. Competition, in this context, is about being better than another, thriving on secrecy, and fostering a spirit of rivalry. But life, at its core, is about being the best you can be, so that others, in turn, can be their best. This individualistic, unhealthy form of competition breeds lust and greed, hindering collaborative work, creating conflict, and ultimately spreading poverty within a community.

Lust, in this context, describes a craving for others' possessions or achievements, leading to immorality, envy, and resentment. It blinds you from recognizing and utilizing your own unique gifts, distracts you from your true purpose, and leads you to actively frustrate others' success. Crucially, lust merely transfers wealth; it does not create it. Similarly, greed inflates egos, creating a false sense of superiority and preventing genuinely helping others for fear they might become more prosperous, thereby threatening your perceived position. Greed views giving as a loss, a depletion of precious resources. Both lust and greed are bitter fruits of unhealthy competition, inhibiting the very acts of giving and serving that are the foundations of true abundance. Without giving and serving, you simply cannot receive or be truly blessed. The fewer blessed people there are in a community, the more immorality and poverty will inevitably prevail.

Conversely, receiving brings growth, both personally and collectively. However, receiving is not a solitary act; it is intrinsically linked to giving. Growth, whether personal or communal, requires a constant exchange—a dynamic flow of resources, ideas, and support. Just as a seed needs rain and sunlight to grow and reach its full potential, so too do individuals and communities need a continuous flow of resources and opportunities. A seed confined to a container, deprived of essential elements, will not grow; it will remain stunted and unproductive.

Thus, giving initiates receiving, creating a powerful cycle of abundance. Your capacity to receive, your ability to experience growth and prosperity, is directly determined by your willingness to give—to share your resources, your talents, and your time. This principle is beautifully expressed in Luke 6:38:

> ***"Give, and it will be given to you. A good measure, pressed down, shaken together and running over, will be poured into your lap. For with the measure you use, it will be measured to you."***

This verse highlights the fundamental principle of reciprocity, illustrating that it is not merely a transactional exchange, but a spiritual law that governs the flow of abundance.

> Further reinforcing this truth, Proverbs 11:24-26 states: ***"One gives freely, yet gains even more; another withholds unduly, but comes to poverty. A generous person will prosper; whoever refreshes others will be refreshed. People curse the one who hoards grain, but a blessing crowns the one who is willing to sell."***

These proverbs highlight the profound importance of generosity and the detrimental effects of hoarding. Those who give freely experience increasing abundance, while those who withhold unjustly face scarcity. Generosity refreshes both the giver and the receiver, creating a perpetual cycle of mutual benefit and collective prosperity.

The Highest Form of Giving

Work, in its essence, is the highest form of giving—a tangible expression of your commitment to serving others and contributing to the world. When approached with purpose and dedication, work transcends the mere exchange of labor for compensation. It becomes a vehicle for service, a conduit for creativity, and a platform for positive impact.

It's the act of investing our time, energy, and talents into a calling that resonates with our values and aspirations, allowing us to make a meaningful contribution to the world.

If you don't give yourself wholeheartedly to your work, if you don't dedicate your time, energy, and talents to your calling, you simply cannot effectively give in other areas of your life. Work isn't merely a means to an end; it's an integral part of who we are, a reflection of our values, and a testament to our commitment to making a difference. It's the foundation upon which we build our lives, the platform from which we launch our contributions to the world.

Diligent work, the consistent application of effort and skill, is always rewarded, both materially and spiritually. These rewards might manifest as financial security, professional recognition, or personal fulfillment. But they also extend beyond the tangible, encompassing the invaluable rewards of self-respect, a profound sense of purpose, and the deep satisfaction of knowing you've positively impacted others.

The wisdom of Proverbs 14:23 highlights the importance of action over words:

> ***"All hard work brings a profit, but mere talk leads only to poverty."***

This proverb highlights the stark contrast between the tangible results of diligent work and the empty promises of idle chatter. Consistent, diligent effort produces tangible results, creating value and generating prosperity. Mere talk, on the other hand, leads to unfulfilled potential and, ultimately, a state of poverty—not just in material terms, but also in personal fulfillment and societal contribution.

Work, therefore, is not a burden to be endured, but a privilege to be embraced. It's an opportunity to express our creativity, utilize our skills, and contribute to the well-being of others. It's a platform for personal growth, a vehicle for social change, and a testament to our commitment to making a difference.

When we approach work with a spirit of service, dedicating ourselves to our calling with passion and purpose, we transform our labor into an act of giving—a profound gift to the world. We create value, solve problems, and inspire others to do the same. We become agents of positive change, contributing to the creation of a more just, equitable, and fulfilling world.

Let's view work as the ultimate act of giving, a powerful force that transforms lives, strengthens communities, and builds a lasting legacy. We should approach our calling with passion and purpose, confident that our efforts will bring both material and spiritual rewards. Ultimately, let's use our work to make a real difference, to serve others, and to help create a world that truly reflects our God-given potential.

The Legacy of Generosity

Just as you have been freely gifted with talents, resources, and knowledge, so too are you called to freely give. Share these blessings with others, contributing actively to their growth and development. Your purpose is to work to be blessed—to create a life not just of personal prosperity, but of profound purpose, widespread abundance, and lasting impact. Imagine your final day being filled with the comforting knowledge that you have genuinely touched countless lives, knowing your legacy is one defined by generosity, selfless service, and love.

> The biblical account of Dorcas powerfully illustrates this principle. Acts 9:36-39 recounts: ***"In Joppa there was a disciple named Tabitha (which, when translated, is Dorcas), who was always doing good and helping the poor... About that time she***

> ***became sick and died... Lydda was near Joppa; so when they heard that Peter was in Lydda, they sent two men to him and urged him, "Please come at once!"... All the widows stood around him, crying and showing him the robes and other clothes that Dorcas had made while she was still with them."***

The story of Dorcas serves as a profound example of the lasting impact of a life dedicated to generosity. Her life was a vibrant testament to her unwavering commitment to serving others, to consciously using her talents—even simple ones like sewing—to alleviate suffering and bring joy. When she died, her loss was felt deeply, not just by her immediate circle, but by an entire community whose lives she had tangibly improved. Her legacy literally lived on in the tangible expressions of her love, seen in the clothing she made, and felt in the hearts of those she had so selflessly helped. Her story compels us to recognize that the true measure of a life is not what we accumulate, but what we give away, and how that giving transforms the lives of others. When we freely give what we have been freely given, we not only fulfill our purpose but also build a legacy that endures far beyond our own time.

The Ripple Effect of Generosity

Life, at its very core, is characterized by the act of generosity. This isn't just about giving material possessions; it's the outpouring of our hearts, the sharing of our time, our talents, and our compassion. True generosity isn't a transactional exchange, but a selfless act of love, a profound recognition of our interconnectedness, and a testament to our commitment to building a better world.

Generosity isn't a solitary act; it's a force that spreads outward, creating a powerful ripple effect that touches countless lives. Imagine a stone thrown into a still pond: it creates concentric circles that expand and spread, reaching far beyond the initial point of impact. Similarly, your acts of kindness, your contributions to your community, and your unwavering commitment to serving others will have a lasting impact, forging a legacy of love and abundance that extends far beyond your own lifetime.

Consider the simple act of sharing a meal with someone in need. This doesn't just provide sustenance; it also offers a sense of connection, a feeling of belonging, and a crucial reminder that they aren't alone. Such an act of kindness can profoundly impact their emotional well-being, giving them hope and strength to face their challenges. Or, reflect on volunteering your time at a local shelter. You're not only providing practical assistance but also offering hope and dignity to those who are struggling. Your presence, your compassion, and your willingness to serve can make a world of difference in their lives.

Generosity isn't limited to grand gestures or large-scale donations. It thrives in the small, everyday acts of kindness we extend to those around us. A kind word, a helping hand, a listening ear—these simple acts can profoundly impact others, creating a ripple effect of positivity that spreads throughout our communities.

Your contributions to your community, whether through volunteering, donating, or simply being a good neighbor, create a legacy of love and abundance that will endure long after you're gone. You're actively building a foundation of compassion, creating a culture of generosity, and inspiring others to follow your example. This legacy isn't about material possessions or worldly recognition; it's about the impact you have on the lives of others, the difference you make in your community, and the love you share with the world. It's about initiating a wave of positivity that transforms lives, strengthens communities, and builds a more just and compassionate world.

Ultimately, generosity isn't a burden, but a profound privilege. It's an opportunity to express our humanity, to connect deeply with others, and to make a meaningful contribution to the world. It is, in itself, a source of joy, fulfillment, and lasting satisfaction.

Let's wholeheartedly embrace the power of generosity, recognizing its ability to transform lives and create a ripple effect of positive change. Let's commit to consistent acts of kindness, dedicated contributions to our communities, and a life truly defined by service. In doing so, we'll create a legacy of love and abundance that will inspire generations to come.

Practical Applications of Giving

Time and Talent:

Volunteer your time and share your talents with those in need.

Financial Resources:

Give generously to charitable causes and support those who are less fortunate.

Knowledge and Wisdom:

Share your knowledge and wisdom with others, mentoring and guiding them on their journey.

Encouragement and Support:

Offer encouragement and support to those who are struggling, lifting them up and inspiring them to persevere.

Acts of Kindness:

Perform acts of kindness, both big and small, bringing joy and comfort to those around you.

Building Community:

Contribute to building strong and supportive communities, fostering a sense of belonging and connection.

Mentorship:

Be a mentor, guide and help others achieve their dreams.

Listen:

Sometimes just listening can be the greatest gift you give.

Forgiveness:

Forgive those who have wronged you. Holding on to the past limits your future ability to give.

7

OVERCOMING THE FEAR OF FAILURE

"They came back to Moses and Aaron and the whole Israelite community at Kadesh in the Desert of Paran. There they reported to them and to the whole assembly and showed them the fruit of the land. They gave Moses this account: "We went into the land to which you sent us, and it does flow with milk and honey! Here is its fruit. But the people who live there are powerful, and the cities are fortified and very large... Then Caleb silenced the people before Moses and said, "We should go up and take possession of the land, for we can certainly do it." But the men who had gone with him said, "We can't attack those people; they are stronger than we are." And they spread among the Israelites a bad report about the land they had explored. They said, "The land we explored devours those living in it. All the people we saw there are of great size... We seemed like grasshoppers in our own eyes, and we looked the same to them." - Numbers 13:26-28, 30-33

The adage, **"Those who fear to fail, start not their venture,"** expresses a fundamental truth about ambition and the pursuit of dreams. It speaks to the paralyzing power of fear, highlighting how it can stifle our potential and prevent us from taking the first steps towards our goals. It highlights the stark reality that the path to achievement is rarely smooth or predictable, and that the willingness to embrace the possibility of failure is a prerequisite for any meaningful endeavor.

The fear of failure, a common human experience, can manifest in a multitude of ways. It can lead to procrastination, the avoidance of challenges, and the creation of elaborate excuses that justify inaction. This fear can create a sense of paralysis, a feeling of being trapped in a cycle of "what ifs" and "maybes," preventing us from ever taking the leap of faith necessary to pursue our dreams. Those who allow fear to dictate their actions often remain in a state of perpetual potential, forever dreaming of what could be, but never daring to take the risks necessary to make those dreams a reality. They become spectators in the grand theater of life, watching others achieve their goals while they remain confined to the sidelines, their talents and abilities left untapped.

To embark on any venture, to pursue any dream, requires a willingness to confront and overcome the fear of failure. It necessitates a shift in perspective, a recognition that failure is not a terminal condition, but rather an integral part of the learning process—a stepping stone on the path to success. It is the understanding that every setback and every mistake provides an opportunity to learn, to grow, and to become stronger.

Those who embrace this perspective understand that failure is not the opposite of success; it is a necessary component of it. They recognize that the greatest failures are not those who stumble and fall, but those who never dare to try. They understand that the only way to guarantee failure is to never take the first step, to never venture beyond the familiar and comfortable.

To start a venture, to pursue a dream, demands courage, resilience, and a willingness to embrace the unknown. It requires self-belief, unwavering commitment to one's goals, and determination to persevere through challenges. It is about understanding that the journey is just as important as the destination, and that the lessons learned along the way are invaluable. It is about recognizing that the potential rewards of success far outweigh the temporary setbacks of failure, and that the deepest regrets stem not from the mistakes we make, but from the opportunities we miss by not trying.

Therefore, let us cultivate a mindset of courage, a willingness to embrace risk, and a determination to pursue our dreams, regardless of the fear of failure. Let us understand that the only way to truly fail is to never try, and that the greatest achievements are often born from the ashes of past setbacks. Let us venture forth, knowing that even if we stumble, we will rise again, stronger and more determined than before. Let us start our ventures, knowing that the journey itself is a victory.

The Psychology of Fear and Failure

Vision involves perceiving your current reality, envisioning your desired future, acknowledging your present state, and understanding the transformation required to reach your destination. It provides a roadmap to success, outlining the steps needed to achieve your goals. However, the fear of failure often arises when you doubt your ability to navigate this roadmap, when you question your capacity to succeed.

Fear of failure is the debilitating feeling that you are incapable of achieving your vision, a mental barrier that obscures your potential and blinds you to the possibilities that lie within reach. Many people remain stagnant, trapped in a cycle of inaction, not because of actual failure, but because of the paralyzing fear of it. People do not truly fear failure itself; if they did, they would not remain complacent, content with their current circumstances. It is the thought of failure, the mental image of defeat, that creates the insurmountable obstacle between you and your success.

The thought of failure is not failure itself. It is merely a mental construct, a perception that can be challenged and overcome. The only way to conquer the fear of failure is to confront it head-on, to refuse to be intimidated by its presence. Failure, in its essence, is indiscriminate, a potential outcome that can affect anyone. If you do not actively confront the thought of failure, it will inevitably conquer you, preventing you from pursuing your dreams and fulfilling your potential. You confront it through preparation, by arming yourself with the knowledge, skills, and resources necessary to succeed.

> ***"Fear is a liar and will steal your dreams if you submit to it. Learn to do what you fear, and the death of fear will be certain." - Anonymous.***

The Mental Battleground

Since your first encounter with failure is through thought, the solution must be mental. Your mission should begin with self-preparation, renewing your mind with faith-inducing knowledge, knowledge that is directly applicable to your goals and aspirations. You need courage, the inner strength to face challenges and overcome obstacles, which comes from self-preparation, from building a foundation of confidence and competence.

Many people remain stagnant, trapped in a state of inaction, because they lack the courage to pursue their vision, paralyzed by the thought of failure. The question "What if I fail?" arises, a persistent voice of doubt that seeks to undermine their confidence. However, they fail to counter this negative thought with the equally valid question, "What if I succeed?" They allow the thought of failure to dominate their thinking, failing to recognize that it is merely a deceptive tactic, a strategy employed to kill their destiny, to prevent them from reaching their full potential.

When the thought of failure arises, assess your mental preparedness. Are you equipped to do what your vision requires? Have you acquired the necessary knowledge and skills? How many options do you have, how many strategies can you employ? By addressing these questions, you can regain control of your thinking and overcome the paralyzing fear of failure.

Learning from Failure: A Pathway to Growth

What do you do when you fail? This question is crucial, for it is not failure itself that defines you, but your response to it. Few people experience failure because few people venture, few people take risks, few people step outside their comfort zones. Those who do venture, those who dare to pursue their dreams, learn that failure does not kill; it teaches you to avoid mistakes, to refine your strategies, and to improve your performance. Learning from mistakes perfects your craft, transforming you into a master of your domain. The greatest failure is the failure to start, to remain stagnant, to allow fear to dictate your actions. He who ventures not, explores not, and gets exploited, remaining trapped in a cycle of mediocrity.

You do not become a failure when you fail; you become a failure when you fail to learn from your mistakes, when you refuse to rise again, and when you surrender to the voice of doubt. Failure is a sign that you tried, that you dared to step outside your comfort zone, that you refused to be limited by your fears. It takes you back to the start, but with new insight and wisdom, with a deeper understanding of your strengths and weaknesses. Success is not achieved overnight; it comes through consistency, through perseverance, through a relentless pursuit of your goals. You have every reason to rise and try again, to learn from your mistakes, and to continue your journey until you succeed. Success speaks loudest at the end, when you have overcome adversity, defied expectations, and achieved your dreams.

The Resilience of Success

A newspaper article about a respected neurosurgeon, Kachinga Sichizya, highlighted his failures. He failed Grade 7, repeated a year in mining school, and another in medical school. But failure didn't stop him. "I have failed more times than anyone I know," he said. "Failure is not final; you can get up again and try a little harder... True strength and courage only come through failure." He later became a global authority on spina bifida and hydrocephalus. (Times of Zambia, June 14, 2008)

This story illustrates the resilience of success, the ability to overcome setbacks and emerge stronger than before. Failure is not the final result; your success depends on your attitude toward failure, your willingness to learn, and your determination to persevere. You were not meant to be overcome by failure; you were designed to overcome it, to learn from it, and to use it as a stepping stone to success. Failing is not quitting; it is merely a temporary setback, a detour on your journey.

Henry Ford's first two car companies failed. The Wright brothers faced countless failures before inventing the airplane. Thomas Edison experimented with numerous filaments before inventing the light bulb. These examples demonstrate that failure is not an indication of impossibility; it is an inevitable part of the journey to success.

Finishing the Race: The Ultimate Triumph

Life, in its unpredictable nature, inevitably presents us with moments of setback, instances where we stumble and fall. Yet, these moments of failure, these temporary detours, don't define our journey. They aren't the final chapter, but rather valuable lessons, opportunities for growth and resilience. Rise if you've fallen, learn from your mistakes, and continue your journey with renewed determination. May you be the one who laughs last, who achieves their dreams, who leaves a lasting legacy—a testament to the power of perseverance and the indomitable spirit of the human heart.

Failing isn't final; finishing is. When you encounter a setback, when you experience a moment of failure, remember that the finish line remains within reach, a beacon of hope illuminating the path ahead. You may stumble, you may falter, but you aren't defeated until you choose to give up. Recall the cloud of witnesses—those who've gone before you, who've faced their own challenges and emerged victorious. They're cheering you on, encouraging you to rise, dust yourself off, and continue the race. They're a reminder that you're not alone, that others have walked this path before you, and that you too can achieve your goals. Get up and finish the race, demonstrating your resilience, determination, and unwavering commitment to your goals. Let your perseverance be a testament to your character, a symbol of your strength, and an inspiration to those who witness your journey.

Don't be embarrassed by failing; embrace it as a valuable learning experience, a stepping stone on the path to success. Every setback is an opportunity to learn, to grow, and to become stronger. Analyze your mistakes, extract the profound lessons they offer, and use them to refine your approach and enhance your performance. If God, the ultimate embodiment of perfection, can do anything but fail, then you, created in His image, endowed with His power, can also do anything but fail. You are more than a conqueror, equipped with the strength, the resilience, and the determination to overcome any obstacle that dares to impede your progress. You have a race to finish, a destiny to fulfill, and a legacy to leave.

The journey may be tough and rough, the challenges daunting, but the reward of finishing—the satisfaction of achieving your goals—is immeasurable. It is in the act of finishing that we demonstrate our true character, our unwavering commitment to our dreams, and our profound belief in our own potential. Therefore, let's embrace the challenges, learn from our mistakes, and persevere through setbacks. Let's run our race with unwavering focus and unwavering determination, knowing that the ultimate triumph lies in crossing the finish line, in fulfilling our destiny, and in leaving a legacy that inspires generations to come. Let us be the ones who finish strong, who achieve our dreams, and who leave a lasting mark on the world.

The Foundation of Unstoppable Belief

The assertion that **"you can do anything but fail"** goes beyond the realm of motivational rhetoric, evolving into a profound declaration anchored in the understanding that you are created in God's image, filled with His great potential. It is a recognition of the divine spark within each individual, the understanding that God has placed within you the capacity for extraordinary achievement, unwavering resilience, and ultimate triumph.

To truly comprehend this concept, it is essential to consider the nature of God's power. It is not a fleeting force, a temporary surge of energy. It is limitless, unwavering, and eternally productive, a constant source of creation and sustenance. God is the ultimate creator, the architect of the universe, the source of all life, and the master of all possibilities. When you acknowledge that you are made in His image, you are acknowledging that you possess a fragment of that creative potential, a spark of that divine power, a reflection of His infinite capacity.

This understanding is not about claiming to be God, but about acknowledging the divine imprint that resides within you. It is about recognizing that you are not a mere accident of circumstance, but a purposeful creation, endowed with unique gifts and talents that reflect the creative power of your maker.

This realization shifts your perspective from a place of limitation to a place of boundless possibility. It empowers you to break free from the shackles of self-doubt, those harmful whispers that tell you "you can't," "you're not good enough," or "it's impossible." It allows you to shed the weight of limiting beliefs, those self-imposed constraints that hold you back from pursuing your dreams and achieving your full potential.

It empowers you to embrace the confidence that comes from knowing you are connected to an infinite source, a source of strength, wisdom, and creativity that transcends your own limitations. It is about understanding that you are not alone in your journey, that you are supported by a power greater than yourself, a power that empowers you to overcome any obstacle, to achieve any goal, and to fulfill your divine purpose.

This is not a license for arrogance or a justification for recklessness. It is a call to humility, a recognition that your abilities are not solely your own, but a gift from your creator. It is a call to responsibility, a reminder that you are accountable for the use of your talents, for the impact you have on the world.

It is a call to faith, a belief that even when you face seemingly insurmountable challenges, you are not alone, that you are equipped with the strength and resilience to persevere. It is a call to action, a reminder that you have a role to play in the unfolding of creation, a purpose to fulfill, and a legacy to leave.

By embracing this understanding, by acknowledging the divine potential within you, you unlock the power to transform your life, to achieve your dreams, and to make a positive impact on the world. You become a living testament to the power of faith, the resilience of the human spirit, and the boundless possibilities that reside within each and every one of us. You become a living embodiment of the truth that you are, indeed, more than a conqueror.

Overcoming Obstacles with Divine Strength

You are not merely capable of surviving the trials that come your way, but of thriving in the midst of them, of finding strength in adversity, and of transforming challenges into opportunities for growth. This concept extends far beyond physical or material victories, beyond the accumulation of wealth or worldly success. It encompasses the entirety of our being—the emotional, mental, and spiritual dimensions of our existence. It is about cultivating an inner strength, a resilience of the soul, that enables us to overcome the internal battles we face, the struggles often unseen by the outside world.

It is about overcoming negative thought patterns—those deceptive whispers of doubt and fear that seek to undermine our confidence and limit our potential. It is about breaking free from limiting beliefs, those self-imposed constraints that hold us back from pursuing our dreams and achieving our goals. It is about cultivating a mindset of unwavering faith, a deep-seated belief in our ability to overcome any obstacle, achieve any goal, and fulfill our God-given purpose.

When faced with adversity, when confronted with challenges that seem insurmountable, remember that you are not alone. You are not a solitary figure battling an overwhelming force. You are equipped with divine strength, with an inner reservoir of power that enables you to persevere, endure, and ultimately triumph. This strength isn't based on your own limited abilities or finite resources; it is based on the unwavering support of the God who created you, who knows your potential, and who empowers you to achieve it.

This divine strength isn't a passive force; it is an active, dynamic energy that flows through you, empowering you to rise above your circumstances, overcome your fears, and achieve your dreams. It is the strength that enables you to transform setbacks into stepping stones, challenges into opportunities, and failures into lessons learned. It is the understanding that you are not defined by your circumstances, but by your response to them. You are not a victim of fate, but a creator of your own destiny. You are not limited by your past, but empowered by your future.

To live as **"more than a conqueror"** is to embrace a mindset of unwavering faith—a belief, with the help of God, that you are capable of achieving anything you set your mind to. It is to cultivate a spirit of resilience, a determination to never give up, and a willingness to learn from your mistakes. It is to recognize that you are not perfect, but that you are perfectly capable of achieving your goals. True strength lies not in the absence of challenges, but in the ability to overcome them. It is to recognize that you are not alone, that you are equipped with divine strength, and that you are capable of achieving anything.

Therefore, let us cultivate a mindset of unwavering faith, and let us live a life that reflects the strength, resilience, and determination that resides within us. Let us overcome our obstacles, achieve our goals, and fulfill our God-given purpose, knowing that we are more than conquerors through Him who loves us.

The Race to Finish: Fulfilling Your Divine Destiny

Life is not a sprint; it's a marathon, a race that requires endurance, perseverance, and unwavering focus.

Your destiny, the culmination of your life's purpose, is not a passive event, a preordained outcome that unfolds without your participation. It's an active pursuit, a dynamic journey demanding your dedication, unwavering belief, and active engagement. It's about taking ownership of your life, making conscious choices, and striving to reach your full potential.

The race to finish is about fulfilling your divine purpose, about using your God-given gifts and talents to make a positive impact on the world. It's about understanding that you're not merely a spectator in the grand theater of life, but an active participant, a contributor to the unfolding narrative of humanity.

This journey, this race to finish, isn't without its challenges. There will be moments of doubt, times when you feel overwhelmed, and instances where you're tempted to give up. But it's in these moments that your perseverance is tested, your resilience strengthened, and your faith deepened. Remember that every setback is an opportunity for growth, every challenge a chance to demonstrate your strength, and every failure a lesson learned. Embrace the obstacles that come your way, knowing they are shaping you, molding you, and preparing you for the fulfillment of your destiny.

The race to finish is not about reaching the finish line first, but about reaching it with integrity, honor, and a sense of accomplishment. It's about running your own race, staying true to your values, and fulfilling your unique purpose. It's about understanding that your journey isn't just for yourself, but for the benefit of others. Your actions, your contributions, and your legacy will inspire those who come after you, encouraging them to pursue their own dreams and to make a positive impact on the world.

The race to finish is about leaving a legacy of hope, a testament to the power of perseverance, and an inspiration to future generations. It's about demonstrating that even in the face of adversity, it's possible to achieve your goals, fulfill your purpose, and make a difference.

Don't wait for destiny to unfold; run toward it with everything you've got. Lace up your shoes, fix your gaze on the finish line, and commit to the relentless pursuit of your God-given purpose. Your legacy begins now.

Practical Applications: Living Out Your Divine Potential

Cultivate a Mindset of Faith:

Regularly affirm your belief in your divine potential. Replace negative thoughts with positive affirmations, focusing on your strengths and abilities.

Embrace Challenges as Opportunities:

View challenges as opportunities for growth and development. Learn from your mistakes, refine your strategies, and emerge stronger than before.

Seek Divine Guidance:

Pray for wisdom, guidance, and strength. Trust that God will lead you on the right path and provide the resources you need to succeed.

Take Action with Confidence:

Step outside your comfort zone and take action towards your goals. Don't let fear paralyze you; embrace the uncertainty and trust in your ability to overcome obstacles.

Persevere Through Setbacks:

Don't let setbacks discourage you. Learn from your mistakes, adjust your course, and keep moving forward.

Celebrate Your Victories:

Acknowledge your achievements, both big and small. Celebrate your progress and reinforce your belief in your ability to succeed.

Serve Others:

Use your gifts and talents to serve others, making a positive impact on the world.

Guard your inner voice:

Do not let the inner critic or the negative voices of others dictate your beliefs.

Practice gratitude:

Be grateful for every step, every lesson, and every opportunity.

The Legacy of Unwavering Belief

When you choose to live out your divine potential, to step into the fullness of your God-given abilities, you become a living embodiment of hope, a beacon of light in a world often shrouded in darkness. You become a tangible example of what's possible when you align your beliefs with your divine purpose, choosing to walk in faith rather than fear, and refusing to allow limitations to define your destiny.

Your life transforms into a powerful narrative—a story of triumph over adversity, a testament to the fact that with God, all things are possible. You demonstrate that setbacks are not roadblocks, but stepping stones; that challenges are not insurmountable obstacles, but opportunities for growth; and that failure is not a final destination, but a temporary detour on the path to success. This inspires others to believe in themselves, to recognize the inherent potential residing within them, and to cultivate the courage to pursue their dreams. You become a catalyst for change, a force for good, and a source of inspiration for those who dare to dream beyond the limitations of their present circumstances.

Your legacy extends beyond merely achieving personal success; it's about empowering others to achieve their own. It's about creating a ripple effect of positivity, a chain reaction of hope, and a culture of belief that permeates your community and extends beyond its borders. You become a living example of how powerful faith can be. You show that belief isn't just about quietly accepting a set of rules; it's an active force that changes what's real, transforms people's lives, and makes amazing things happen. You prove that faith isn't naive; instead, it's visionary, offering a clear view of what's not yet seen and a strong confidence in the good things that are coming.

Moreover, your life becomes a testament to the resilience of the human spirit, demonstrating that even in the face of overwhelming odds, it's possible to rise above adversity, to overcome challenges, and to emerge stronger and more determined than before. You show that the human spirit isn't fragile, but resilient, capable of enduring hardship and triumphing over tribulation. Your legacy of unwavering belief is a gift to the world, a treasure that will continue to inspire and empower generations to come. It's a reminder that we are all capable of achieving extraordinary things, that we are all created with a purpose, and that with God, all things are possible.

Let's strive to live lives worthy of this legacy—lives that embody the power of faith, the resilience of the human spirit, and an unwavering belief in the potential for good. Step into your divine potential today; let your life be the light that ignites hope in others, proving that extraordinary is within reach for everyone.

IV

PART D: The True Engines of Productivity

Money: A Secondary Tool

8

TIME: THE ULTIMATE RESOURCE

"The race is not to the swift or the battle to the strong, nor does food come to the wise or wealth to the brilliant or favor to the learned; but TIME and opportunity happen to them all!" - Ecclesiastes 9:11

Time: The Fundamental Currency of Productivity

Contrary to popular belief, money is not the primary driver of productivity. Like many tools we utilize to enhance our lives, it is a secondary resource. The notion that **"you use money to make money"** is a flawed and exclusionary concept. It implies that those without financial resources are inherently incapable of altering their circumstances, trapped in a cycle of poverty. This belief has tragically permeated the lives of countless individuals worldwide, hindering their potential and perpetuating cycles of despair.

The reality is that time, not money, is the fundamental resource used to generate wealth. Money is an asset, a byproduct of the wise investment of time, talent, and effort. Without time's relentless passage, there can be no production, no creation, no achievement. It is the bedrock upon which all productivity is built—the canvas on which we paint our dreams, the clay we mold into our realities. Every invention, thriving business, meaningful relationship, honed skill, and notable accomplishment is built upon the foundation of time invested.

The Asset Characteristics of Money

Money possesses distinct asset characteristics:

- It has a price: It can be bought, sold, and traded for goods and services.
- It can be stored: It can be saved and accumulated for future use.
- It is subject to appreciation or depreciation: Its value fluctuates due to economic factors.
- It is transferable: It can be exchanged between individuals.
- It is subject to control: Its use can be managed strategically.

Yet, despite these attributes, money remains subservient to time and effort.

The Subservient Nature of Money

While it is often said that **"money answers all things,"** it is crucial to understand that money answers to work. It is the output of productive labor, the reward for value creation. Money is a tool—and like any tool, it is only effective when wielded with skill and intention.

Money can be either an asset or a liability, depending on its impact on your life. It can bring happiness and security, or it can lead to misery and anxiety. The determining factor is not the amount possessed, but how it is acquired and utilized.

Money can purchase possessions, but it cannot guarantee success. True success is not defined by material wealth, but by personal growth, meaningful contributions, and the fulfillment of one's purpose. It is through these achievements that wealth naturally follows. You become rich because you are successful, not successful because you are rich. Success is the cause; wealth is the effect.

The Great Equalizer: Time

Time is the universal currency—the great equalizer. We all receive the same 24 hours each day; no one controls its flow or can manipulate its passage. While it is not scarce in its daily arrival, it is definitively finite. Like manna in the wilderness, it is only enough for the present moment—it cannot be stored, borrowed, or bought.

At birth, our lives are like a blank, signed cheque with an instruction note: **"Any amount is possible."** You fill the cheque of your life by what you do with time. Every moment is an opportunity to invest wisely or let it slip away. If we neglect our time, the "cheque" of our potential may go unfulfilled, leaving behind regret and unrealized possibilities.

> We enter this world with nothing but time, and it ultimately shapes our legacy. As Ecclesiastes 3:1 reminds us, ***"To everything there is a season, and a time to every purpose under the heavens."***

Productivity, success, and wealth are not born from money—they are born from the disciplined, purposeful investment of time.

The Dual Nature of Time: Factor and Resource

Time holds a dual nature, acting both as an external force that influences our lives and an internal tool we can actively wield. It's a constant presence, shaping our experiences whether we acknowledge it or not, yet it's also a valuable resource we can consciously manage.

As an external force, time establishes the rhythm of our existence.

It dictates the start and end of our days, shapes the flow of our weeks, and defines the larger cycles of seasons and years. It's like an unseen current, consistently guiding our lives whether we're aware of it or not.

But time is also a valuable resource—something precious we can actually use. We use it every day, we decide how to spend it, we put it into things that help us grow, and we use it smartly to reach our goals. It's really important to see time in both these ways: as a force that shapes our lives, but also as something we can actively manage.

To really get the most out of time, we need to make it our friend, our helper, our partner. This means we have to really understand how it affects us and then plan how we're going to use it. Think about it: time is literally all you have to build your life on. Every dream, every success, every relationship—they all happen within the boundaries of time. If you waste it, you're not just losing a few minutes; you're losing out on your potential and what you're meant to achieve in life. By treating time as a true partner, we can ride its waves while still steering our own ship.

Let's unpack the dual nature of time, emphasizing its critical importance:

Time as a Factor (External Force):

Time dictates the rhythm of our days, weeks, and years. It sets the deadlines, the seasons, the natural cycles that influence our activities.

It's the framework within which events unfold, the stage upon which we play out our lives.

We cannot alter its passage; we can only adapt to it. This necessitates understanding its influence and aligning ourselves with its flow.

It's the steady beat that sets the pace for everything we do.

Wealth isn't always created by toilsome labor, by sheer physical exertion. It doesn't have to come from sheer brute force or constant, tiring effort. Instead, it's often about working smarter with the time you already have.

> ***"It is not necessary that a man should earn his living by the sweat of his brow." - Henry David Thoreau.***

Time as a Resource (Internal Tool):

Time is a limited resource that we can choose to spend, invest, and make use of. It's like any other valuable possession that needs to be managed well. We have the power to decide how we use our time, what activities we focus on, and what dreams we chase. In essence, time is the very stuff we use to build our lasting impact.

We can actively choose to put our time into learning new things, strengthening relationships, or following our deepest interests. Managing time effectively means deciding what's most important, setting clear goals, and getting rid of things that distract us. By being mindful about how we use our time, we can truly shape our lives and achieve what we aspire to.

Time as a Determinant:

As a determinant, time exerts its influence through external factors such as work schedules, family commitments, and societal expectations, all of which operate on its defined rhythms. The natural progression of days and seasons similarly dictates fundamental activities like planting and harvesting, periods of work, and times of rest. By understanding this external influence, we are better able to plan and adapt, thereby minimizing friction and maximizing our efficiency within its unyielding framework.

Understanding Time's Influence:

To truly understand time's influence, it's vital to observe the natural rhythms of your own life and adjust your activities to match them. You should recognize the limitations that time imposes and plan what you do within those boundaries. It's also important to be aware of the different "seasons" of life, knowing when to shift your expectations and activities to suit each one.

Mastering Time: Harnessing Its Power

When it comes to planning how you use your time, it's smart to create schedules and to-do lists. These tools help you decide what's most important and how to best use your available time. You should also set clear goals and then break them down into smaller, manageable steps that have deadlines. To make the most of your time, get rid of distractions and focus only on activities that truly help you reach your goals. It's also wise to invest your time in activities that will benefit you in the long run.

Building a good relationship with time means seeing it as a valuable friend, not something you're constantly fighting against. Develop a deep respect for time and understand that it's a limited resource you can't get back. Learn to truly appreciate the present moment and make the absolute most of each day you have.

Discernment and careful planning are crucial. You need to develop the skill to tell the difference between activities that are genuinely important and those that are just busywork. Always prioritize tasks that align with your core values and overall goals. By planning your time strategically, you'll ensure you're putting your efforts into activities that will give you the greatest rewards.

The Ultimate Consequence:

Wasting time is equivalent to wasting life itself.

Every moment squandered is a missed opportunity to create, to learn, to grow.

Time is the only truly irreplaceable resource, and its loss is irreversible.

The way we use our time, is the way we craft our life.

> ***"As if you could kill time without injuring eternity." - Henry Daniel Thoreau***

To create wealth, to achieve prosperity, you must understand **TIME**, the rhythm of life, the flow of opportunity. Everything we do unfolds within its framework. A profound grasp of time means working smartly, strategically, and efficiently, rather than just toiling endlessly. Simply being busy without understanding time is a futile exercise, a meaningless pursuit of activity without true purpose.

Understanding time means recognizing the opportune moment for every action and seizing fleeting chances. Success often hinges on doing the right things at the right time. As Ecclesiastes 8:6a wisely states,

> ***"For there is a proper time and procedure for every matter."***

Your prosperity is directly linked to how effectively you utilize this invaluable resource. Effective time management is, in essence, effective life management—a disciplined approach that maximizes your potential and helps you achieve your goals. Conversely, squandering time robs you of future opportunities and hinders your progress. Investing time wisely, however, rewards you with abundance and a life rich in purpose and fulfillment. Shape your present choices with an eye on your desired future, for tomorrow is truly a harvest of today.

Many people are careful with their money, carefully managing every penny, yet they thoughtlessly squander their time on trivial pursuits. This oversight is critical, as time is far more valuable than money. While money can be lost and regained, time, once spent, is gone forever. You cannot buy time with money, but through wise investments and strategic efforts, time can certainly generate wealth.

Therefore, be incredibly mindful of how you spend each moment, for every second is precious and irreplaceable. Plan each day, hour, and minute, ensuring your activities align with your goals and contribute to your broader vision. Wasting time is akin to undermining your own destiny, preventing you from reaching your full potential. Time cannot be stored or replenished; it's a fleeting resource that demands wise utilization. Learn to discern the unspoken signals and gentle nudges of time, allowing them to guide you toward your true purpose.

Time's Speech: The Language of Opportunity

Time "talks" to us all the time, not with words, but through simple things: the switch from day to night, the way nature cycles through seasons, and the natural rhythm of life itself. We should plan our daily activities to go along with this natural flow, instead of fighting against it. Make sure not to let a day pass without doing something valuable—something that helps you grow, or moves you closer to your dreams. Remember, time itself doesn't magically change things; you change your life with it, through the choices you make, the actions you take, and how dedicated you are to what you want to achieve. As the wise saying from the Psalms puts it,

> ***"Day unto day utters speech, And night unto night reveals knowledge. There is no speech nor language where their voice is not heard. Their line has gone out through all the earth, And their words to the end of the world," - Psalm 19:2-4.***

This means time is always sending us silent, universal messages.

Time isn't just a continuous flow; it operates in natural cycles, much like seasons. These natural rhythms guide everything from agriculture to personal well-being. To truly thrive, we must align ourselves with these cycles, working in harmony with their natural flow. This alignment fosters balance and leads to optimal outcomes.

Just as a farmer understands the precise timing for planting and harvesting, we too need to recognize the "seasons" within our own lives. This discerning awareness allows us to act at the opportune moment. As the timeless wisdom of Ecclesiastes 3:1 reminds us,

> ***"To everything there is a season."***

Understanding and respecting these natural rhythms is paramount for effective living and achieving genuine abundance. The sons of Issachar, noted in 1 Chronicles 12:32, were praised because they **"had understanding of the times, to know what Israel ought to do."** Similarly, by learning to **"number our days"** as encouraged in Psalms 90:12, we can **"gain a heart of wisdom,"** empowering us to navigate life's seasons with insight and purpose.

The Divide of Time: Preparation and Rest

Life can be broadly understood as having two distinct periods: the former and the latter. The former is the season for wealth creation through diligent work, for actively building a strong foundation, and for sowing the crucial seeds of your future. How you live through this initial phase, the way you invest your time and energy, directly determines the quality of the latter period. The latter period is intended for rest, for enjoying the rewards of your previous labor, and for savoring the fruits of your efforts. It's truly tragic to enter this stage without having made provisions, without a secure foundation of stability and abundance. This unfortunate situation often befalls those who treated time frivolously, squandered opportunities, and failed to adequately prepare for what lies ahead. The fundamental principle is clear: work must precede rest, and effort must precede reward. Attempting to rest before putting in the work is simply laziness, a self-defeating approach that inevitably leads to regret and scarcity. As John Ruskin aptly put it, **"Work first and then rest."**

> Ancient wisdom reinforces this truth. Proverbs 10:5 states, ***"He who gathers crops in summer is a wise son, but he who sleeps during harvest is a disgraceful son."***

This timeless advice highlights the importance of timely action and diligence. The book of Proverbs further illustrates this point with the humble ant:

> ***"Go to the ant, you sluggard; consider its ways and be wise! It has no commander, no overseer or ruler; yet it stores up its provisions in summer and gathers its food at harvest. How long will you lie there, you sluggard? When will you get up from your sleep? A little sleep, a little slumber; a little folding of the hands to rest—and poverty will come on you like a bandit and scarcity like an armed man." (Proverbs 6:6–11).***

Even **"Ants are creatures of little strength, yet they store up their**

food in the summer" (Proverbs 30:25), demonstrating that foresight and consistent effort, regardless of one's natural strength, are key to preventing future hardship.

Consider the illustration of a seed: the seed you consume today offers only temporary gratification, but it simultaneously deprives you of future abundance. In contrast, the seed you plant becomes your harvest, a strategic investment that yields a bountiful return over time. Seeds are fundamentally for planting, for investing in the future, not for immediate consumption. As Emerson wisely noted, **"The sum of wisdom is that the time is never lost that is devoted to work."** Similarly, the sentiment that **"Work is time-consuming but never time-wasting"** and C. M. Schwab's assertion that **"Hard work is the best investment a man can make"** highlights the profound value of effort. These insights collectively emphasize that purposeful labor in the "former" period of life is not just about earning a living, but about cultivating a secure and fulfilling "latter" period.

Redeeming Time: The Power of Today

It is absolutely critical to never miss the next season, to never squander the present opportunity that time offers. While the past is unchangeable in itself, the good news is that time can be redeemed, meaning that past mistakes can be corrected through present actions, and futures can indeed be transformed. In what might be thought of as God's divine calendar, there is Yesterday, Today, and Tomorrow. Of these, the greatest and most pivotal is undeniably Today—the present moment. It is this very moment that holds the power and the opportunity to make a tangible difference in your life. Use today to rectify the errors of yesterday, to truly learn from past failures, and to proactively brighten your tomorrow by taking decisive action right now. The profound truth is that you can only genuinely live for today, as it is the sole moment you truly possess. As Matthew 6:34 wisely states, **"Sufficient for the day is the trouble thereof,"** emphasizing the importance of focusing on the present.

Therefore, it's essential to trap time, to seize the moment with deliberate intent. Turn this captured moment into genuine wealth, into lasting abundance, and into a legacy of meaningful impact. Invest today with purpose; sow seeds of opportunity with every action you take. Your aim should be to prepare diligently for the latter part of your life so that it can be the absolute **BEST**—truly the **REST** of your life, a period characterized by profound fulfillment, immense joy, and deep peace. This kind of investment, however, demands delayed gratification. It means consciously sacrificing immediate, fleeting pleasures for the sake of greater, long-term rewards. It's about sowing diligently today, knowing that the bountiful harvest of tomorrow depends entirely on the seeds you plant in the present. This active, conscious engagement with time transforms it from a mere passage of moments into a powerful tool for shaping your destiny.

Practical Applications of Time Management

Prioritize Tasks:

Identify and focus on high-impact activities.

Set Time Blocks:

Allocate specific time slots for important tasks.

Eliminate Distractions:

Minimize interruptions and create a focused work environment.

Delegate Tasks:

Empower others to handle tasks that don't require your direct involvement.

Learn to Say No:

Protect your time by declining non-essential commitments.

Plan Your Day:

Create a daily schedule and stick to it.

Reflect and Evaluate:

Regularly assess your time management strategies and make adjustments as needed.

Use Tools and Technology:

Leverage apps and software to streamline your workflow.

Rest and Recharge:

Schedule breaks and prioritize self-care to maintain productivity.

Maintain a Time Journal:

Track how you spend your time to gain insights and identify areas for improvement.

Embrace the Power of the Present:

Focus on the "now" and do not dwell too much on the past or future.

The Legacy of Time Well Spent

By truly mastering the art of time management, you gain the power to craft a life that is rich in purpose, overflowing with fulfillment, and leaves behind a lasting impact on the world. This isn't just about getting more done; it's about strategically channeling your energy and efforts to build a remarkable legacy of achievement that stands the test of time.

When you manage your time effectively, you set an example. Your focused dedication can inspire others around you to recognize their own potential and strive for greatness. You become a beacon, showing what's possible when time is treated as a precious ally. Ultimately, by consistently making wise choices with your time, you contribute to something larger than yourself, actively leaving the world a better place than you found it.

In essence, time isn't just a component of your life; it is your most valuable asset. Unlike money, it cannot be replaced or recovered once spent. Therefore, using it wisely is the single most critical decision you can make. Do so, and you will undoubtedly reap a bountiful harvest, not just of material abundance, but of meaningful experiences, profound satisfaction, and a life truly well-lived.

9

OPPORTUNITY: THE ART OF ADAPTATION

"The race is not to the swift or the battle to the strong, nor does food come to the wise or wealth to the brilliant or favor to the learned; but time and OPPORTUNITY happen to them all." - Ecclesiastes 9:11

"No great man ever complains of want of opportunity." - Emerson

It's a common saying that **"Opportunities are missed for lack of nothing but self-preparation."** This powerful idea truly highlights how important it is for us to be ready if we want to grab the chances life throws our way. It suggests that while the world is full of amazing possibilities, many of us simply aren't prepared enough internally to take advantage of them.

The truth is, opportunities are everywhere. The world is always changing, constantly offering us new chances to learn, grow, and reach our goals. These might pop up as new job openings, exciting business ideas, chances to further our education, or even experiences that help us grow as people. However, these golden opportunities often require us to have specific skills, knowledge, or experiences. If we haven't put in the effort to get ready, we might find ourselves completely unprepared to seize them, letting them simply slip through our fingers. This idea puts the ball squarely in our court; it tells us that our success isn't just about what happens around us, but largely about how willing we are to work on ourselves. The sad result of ignoring this self-preparation is a life filled with missed chances, "what ifs," and deep regrets. It's a stark reminder that our potential will stay just like that—potential—without the necessary groundwork.

This brings us to an even more inspiring thought:

> ***"When opportunity meets with self-preparation, it is called favor."***

This isn't just a clever phrase; it points to the amazing power that happens when opportunity and readiness come together. It suggests that when we've done our homework and are truly prepared, opportunities don't just feel like random chances; they feel like moments of pure luck or even a kind of special blessing. When we've put in the effort to develop our skills, gain knowledge, and gather experience, we are perfectly positioned to jump on opportunities when they appear. We're not caught off guard; instead, we're ready to embrace the challenge and enjoy the rewards. This idea of "favor" suggests a kind of divine blessing or fortunate timing, as if everything aligns perfectly to support our success when we are ready. It also implies that what might seem like pure chance is often the direct result of our own careful preparation. In other words, we often create our own "luck" by investing in ourselves and putting ourselves in the best position to succeed. When opportunity truly meets self-preparation, our potential is amplified, allowing us to achieve more than we ever thought possible and creating a powerful sense of momentum and fulfillment in our lives.

Ultimately, these ideas serve as a strong reminder that preparation isn't just a one-time event; it's an ongoing process that demands dedication and commitment. Opportunities often come disguised, so we need to be vigilant and sharp to spot them. And finally, "favor" isn't just handed out; it's something we earn through our hard work and readiness. By truly embracing the importance of getting ourselves prepared, we can transform our lives from a series of missed chances into a continuous journey of growth and achievement.

Opportunity: The Intersection of Time and Adaptation

In the previous chapter, we explored time as the raw material for productivity. Building on that foundation, we now delve into opportunity, a time-related concept crucial for success. Opportunity is not a static entity; instead, it's a dynamic interplay between time, change, and adaptation.

Every season brings change, and every change holds potential—a seed of opportunity waiting to be cultivated. Change is an inevitable, constant force that shapes our lives and environments. To succeed, we must adapt to these changes, respond proactively, and leverage them to our advantage. Failure to adapt is catastrophic, leading to stagnation, irrelevance, and ultimately, failure.

Opportunity, then, is the deliberate adaptation to environmental changes in line with your vision—a strategic response that transforms challenges into stepping stones. Every circumstance and every situation demands a proactive response that turns adversity into advantage. Just as a storm doesn't rage according to a ship's size, nor does turbulence depend on an airplane's model, it's the captain's and pilot's responsibility to navigate, adapt to changing conditions, and steer their vessel to safety. You are designed for success, equipped with the resilience and adaptability necessary to overcome any challenge.

While seasons bring change, opportunity means making that change beneficial, transforming it into a catalyst for growth and achievement. Your effectiveness—your ability to thrive in a dynamic environment—is determined by your adaptability, your capacity to respond effectively to changing circumstances. You constantly interact with your environment, drawing resources, leveraging opportunities, and contributing products that meet the needs of society. Adaptability allows you to leverage available resources, harness the power of change, and meet societal needs in innovative ways.

Ultimately, changes are meant to make you work, stimulate your creativity, and challenge your abilities, not to hinder or paralyze you with fear. Idleness is detrimental, a breeding ground for stagnation and regret. Success is simply the sum of seized opportunities, the accumulation of strategic choices that transform challenges into triumphs. These opportunities consistently arise from environmental changes—from life's constant shifts.

The Omnipresence of Opportunity

Opportunity is fundamentally time-related, directly linked to the very flow of life. Where there's time, there's opportunity—a constant stream of possibilities waiting to be discovered. This holds true for everyone, regardless of their background, status, or abilities; opportunity isn't a rare stroke of luck or a fleeting moment of fortune. Many mistakenly wait for someone to "give" them an opportunity, to simply bestow upon them a chance for success. However, like time itself, opportunity isn't subject to anyone's will or controlled by external forces. Instead, it hinges on your perception, your mindset, and your interaction with your environment. Greatness abounds with opportunities, but it requires a positive mindset, a proactive approach, and a willingness to see possibilities where others see obstacles. Every situation, every circumstance, presents an opportune moment for something—a potential catalyst for growth and achievement.

> It's right to say that ***"things turn out best for the people who make the best of the way things turn out."***

This insightful statement beautifully highlights several key aspects of navigating life. It acknowledges that life is often unpredictable; things rarely go exactly as planned. We're frequently faced with changing circumstances and unexpected events beyond our control. Because of this, adaptability is key. The ability to adjust to these shifts and find the positive even in difficult situations is crucial for both success and happiness.

Furthermore, our mindset matters immensely. Our attitude toward challenges significantly shapes how we experience and overcome them. This highlights our fundamental ability to act and our responsibility; we have the power to choose how we react to the circumstances we encounter. We aren't just passive recipients of fate but active participants in shaping our own journey. This principle encourages us to focus on the positive, to find the good in any situation, and to maximize the opportunities that arise, even amidst adversity. By consistently making the best of tough situations, we develop resilience and foster growth, learning valuable lessons along the way. Ultimately, this highlights the immense power of perspective. Often, it's not the event itself, but how we choose to view it, that truly determines our experience. By opting to see the positive, we can transform challenges into genuine opportunities.

In essence, it's vital to embrace the uncertainty of life and cultivate a flexible and adaptable mindset. This means consistently focusing on solutions rather than dwelling on problems, and striving to find the good in every situation, no matter how challenging. Ultimately, we must take responsibility for our own happiness. This serves as a powerful reminder that while we may not be able to control everything that happens to us, we undeniably control how we respond. And in the end, it is precisely our response that determines the outcome.

Consider two people walking through the same environment, experiencing the same circumstances. One sees only dirt, a barren landscape, a symbol of hardship. The other sees building materials, a foundation for creation, a source of potential. Opportunity is all about your perception of your environment—your ability to see possibilities where others see limitations. Every situation holds an opportunity, a chance to create value, to solve problems, and to make a difference. Opportunity refers to the efficient use of time for optimal gratification, for maximizing your potential and achieving your goals. It's a conjunction of circumstances requiring your effort, your talent, and your unwavering commitment. Life is a package of possibilities, a collection of opportunities waiting to be explored. To seize your opportunity, you must choose what aligns with your destiny, what resonates with your purpose, and what contributes to your vision.

> As 1 Corinthians 10:23 wisely states, ***"Everything is permissible—but not everything is beneficial. Everything is permissible—but not everything is constructive."***

Seizing opportunity requires sacrifice, a willingness to prioritize your goals, and to invest your time and energy wisely. Choose how to invest your skills, talents, and time, ensuring that your actions align with your values and contribute to your long-term vision. Not all gratification is truly fulfilling, and not all pleasures lead to lasting satisfaction. Choose wisely, for you have limited time—a finite resource that must be utilized strategically. Knowledge helps you choose correctly, providing the wisdom and discernment necessary to make informed decisions. Effective time management is essential, ensuring that you allocate your time effectively and maximize your productivity.

Opportunity Embedded in Challenges

Many miss opportunities due to slothful thinking, expecting easy solutions, waiting for shortcuts. Opportunity is work, often embedded in needs, problems, or crises, requiring effort, dedication, and perseverance.

> ***"Opportunity is missed by most people because it is dressed in overalls and looks like work." - Author unknown***
>
> ***"Opportunities don't come in the package we are used to; most times they come disguised with the dust of simplicity and the stare of the ordinary. This is what makes opportunities difficult to see when they come." - Happy Mulwe***
>
> ***"Opportunities are seldom labeled." - John A. Shield***

Opportunity is a call to action, a summons to respond to the needs of the world. God's opportunity for creation was a chaotic earth (see Genesis 1:2), a blank canvas upon which He painted His masterpiece. Your opportunity is embedded in your problems, in the challenges you face, in the needs you see around you. Solve them, address them, and you will unlock your potential, reveal your greatness. Examples:

JOSEPH: Pharaoh's dream needed interpretation (Genesis 41:1, 8, 14-16, 25, 39-40, 44).

DAVID: Goliath's challenge needed a response (1 Samuel 17:23-24, 26-27, 32).

DANIEL: Nebuchadnezzar's dream needed interpretation (Daniel 2:1-4, 9c-12, 24-28, 46, 48).

Problems are incubators for greatness, fertile ground for innovation and achievement. Opportunity is not an easy way out, a shortcut to success, but a way out of problems, a path to overcoming challenges and creating solutions.

> ***"God is faithful, and he will not allow you to have a trial or suffer beyond your strength, but with every trial he also provides the way of escape, an opportunity, so that you may be able to endure the trial." – 1 Corinthians 10:13 (Author's paraphrase)***
>
> ***"In the middle of difficulty lies opportunity." – Albert Einstein***

Life is full of possibilities, a design of opportunities waiting to be woven into a masterpiece. Solve problems, address needs, and you will reveal your greatness, unleash your potential, and fulfill your destiny. Your background, your experiences, your circumstances, hold opportunity, a unique perspective, a valuable contribution. Ask:

- What do you see around you?
- What do you think about what you see?

Every situation is an opportunity, a chance to make a difference, to create value, to leave a legacy. You can be what you choose, but you are meant to be a ruler, a leader, a creator. Time presents opportunities, a constant flow of possibilities. Work what you can, utilize your talents, leverage your resources. Seize your birthright of success, your inherent potential for greatness.

The Proactive Pursuit of Opportunity

Opportunity happens to all, but is seized by those who seek it, by those who are proactive, by those who are vigilant.

> ***"A wise man will make more opportunities than he finds." – Bacon***

> ***"Those who wait for opportunities NEVER see them land at their airport of expectation." - Happy Mulwe***
>
> ***"The world is not for the idle. There is no opportunity that is identified by the lazy." - Chibamba Kanyama***
>
> ***"Laziness brings on deep sleep, and the idle man goes hungry." - Proverbs 19:15***

Those who wait for perfect conditions, for ideal circumstances, never find them, remaining trapped in a cycle of inaction.

"Whoever watches the wind will not plant; whoever looks at the clouds will not reap." - Ecclesiastes 11:4

"The sluggard will not plow by reason of the cold; so at harvest time he looks but finds nothing." - Proverbs 20:4

> ***"Don't wait; seek opportunities, pursue them with passion, with determination, with unwavering focus. Don't wait for things to happen; make them happen, create your own opportunities, shape your own destiny."***

This statement is a direct challenge to inactivity and a resounding endorsement of proactive engagement with life. It's a declaration of self-agency and a recipe for taking control of one's future.

This philosophy begins with a clear rejection of inactivity, immediately dispelling the notion of passively waiting for life to unfold. Instead, it emphasizes proactive action, urging us to actively search for opportunities, to be vigilant and observant, and to recognize potential where others might see none. It encourages the cultivation of initiative, fostering a willingness to step outside our comfort zones and take calculated risks.

The statement further instructs us to **"pursue them with passion, with determination, with unwavering focus."** This highlights the importance of infusing our efforts with passion, allowing enthusiasm and zeal to fuel our drive. It highlights the necessity of unwavering determination, the resolute ability to persevere through obstacles and setbacks. And crucial to it all is the power of focus, maintaining concentration, avoiding distractions, and staying committed to our goals.

The directive, **"Don't wait for things to happen; make them happen,"** reinforces the rejection of a passive, fatalistic outlook—the belief that life is solely determined by external forces. Instead, it promotes a strong sense of self-efficacy, a belief in our own ability to influence circumstances and shape our destiny. This encourages a vital shift from merely reacting to events to actively creating them, moving from being a follower to being a leader. Ultimately, to **"create your own opportunities, shape your own destiny,"** speaks to the power of innovation—finding new ways to forge paths where none existed before. It highlights the profound responsibility of self-determination, reminding us that we are ultimately accountable for shaping our own lives. This empowers individuals to take control of their destinies, to live lives filled with purpose and meaning, and to leave a lasting legacy.

In essence, this statement serves as a powerful reminder that life is not a spectator sport. Opportunities aren't always handed out; they are often created. Passion, determination, and focus are indispensable ingredients for success, and we genuinely have the power to shape our own destinies. It is a compelling call to embrace a proactive, empowered approach to life, to seize the initiative, and to create the future we desire. As Ecclesiastes 11:6 advises,

> ***"In the morning sow your seed and in the evening withhold not your hand: for you do not know which shall prosper, either this or that, or whether they both shall be alike good."***

Similarly, Proverbs 20:13 warns,

> ***"Do not love sleep or you will grow poor: stay awake and you will have food to spare,"***

and Ecclesiastes 9:10 encourages,

> ***"Whatsoever your hand finds to do, do it with your might."***

The Art of Opportunity Recognition

Opportunity recognition is a skill honed through observation, critical thinking, and a proactive mindset. It involves:

Environmental Scanning:

Paying close attention to trends, needs, and changes in your surroundings.

Problem Identification:

Recognizing challenges and seeing them as potential opportunities for solutions.

Creative Thinking:

Generating innovative ideas and approaches to address problems and create value.

Risk Assessment:

Evaluating the potential rewards and risks associated with each opportunity.

Action Bias:

Taking decisive action and implementing your ideas.

Cultivating an Opportunity Mindset

Stay Curious:

Maintain a sense of wonder and a desire to learn new things.

Embrace Change:

View change as an opportunity for growth and innovation.

Develop Problem-Solving Skills:

Practice identifying and solving problems in your daily life.

Build a Network:

Connect with people from diverse backgrounds and perspectives.

Take Calculated Risks:

Be willing to step outside your comfort zone and try new things.

Learn from Failure:

View setbacks as learning opportunities and use them to refine your strategies.

Maintain a Positive Attitude:

Cultivate a belief in your ability to create opportunities and achieve your goals.

Practice Gratitude:

Appreciate the opportunities that come your way and express gratitude for them.

The Legacy of Seized Opportunities

Those who possess the vision and the audacity to seize opportunities, to recognize the potential hidden within challenges, leave behind a legacy that echoes through time. They are the architects of progress, the builders of bridges, the creators of solutions, the problem solvers who shape the world around them, leaving an indelible mark on the landscape of human achievement.

They are the innovators who dare to challenge the status quo, the entrepreneurs who transform ideas into realities, and the leaders who inspire others to reach their full potential. They are the ones who see possibilities where others see limitations, who dare to dream beyond the confines of conventional thinking, and who possess the courage to translate their visions into tangible results.

By cultivating an opportunity mindset, a perspective that sees challenges as stepping stones and setbacks as learning experiences, and by taking proactive action, by refusing to be passive observers and instead becoming active participants in shaping their own destinies, you can transform your life and make a lasting difference.

It's about understanding that opportunities are not always presented on a silver platter; they often require us to dig deep, to seek them out, and to create them where they don't readily exist. It's about recognizing that the greatest opportunities often lie hidden within the most challenging circumstances.

It's about understanding that our impact is not limited by our circumstances, but by our willingness to act. It's about recognizing that we all have the potential to make a positive difference in the world, to leave a legacy that inspires and empowers others.

V

PART E: The Imperative of Action

"How long will you wait before you begin to take possession of the land that the LORD, the God of your fathers, has given you?" (Joshua 18:3). This question, posed to the Israelites, resonates with a timeless urgency, a call to action that echoes through generations. It speaks to the danger of procrastination, the folly of waiting for perfect circumstances, and the necessity of seizing the present moment.

10

A CALL TO ACTION AND LEGACY

The compelling story of the four lepers at the city gate in 2 Kings 7:3-5 offers a powerful lesson on the human condition.

> ***"Now there were four leprous men at the entrance of the gate; and they said to one another, 'Why are we sitting here until we die? If we say, 'We will enter the city,' the famine is in the city, and we shall die there. And if we sit here, we die also. Now therefore, come, let us surrender to the army of the Syrians. If they keep us alive, we shall live; and if they kill us, we shall only die.' And they rose at twilight to go to the camp of the Syrians; and when they had come to the outskirts of the Syrian camp, to their surprise no one was there."***

Faced with certain death, they chose action over despair, a courageous step that led to their unexpected salvation. This biblical account perfectly illustrates a vital truth: we must actively pursue our visions, moving beyond the paralyzing grip of fear and doubt, and embracing the transformative power of taking action.

The Barrenness of Inaction

It's simply impossible to truly please God without practically demonstrating what you believe. Idle talk is cheap; those who do nothing but complain often lead unfulfilled lives. As the saying goes, **"Faith, without works, is barren."** Similarly, a vision without implementation remains a mere fantasy. The world is full of grand ideas that never become reality. Real fulfillment isn't found in just talking about dreams, but in relentlessly working to make them happen. Indeed,

> ***"A look at the map of success will definitely show you that the road to success passes through the land of action."***

Success isn't a place you passively arrive at; it's a journey you actively undertake, filled with challenges, obstacles, and detours. Only by stepping onto this path of action can you hope to achieve your aspirations.

Launching into the Deep

> ***"Those who catch fish don't fish from the shore but launch out into the deep."***

Comfort zones are like stagnant pools, breeding complacency. To truly thrive, you must be willing to venture beyond what's familiar, embracing the uncertainties of the unknown. This requires courage, resilience, and a willingness to explore uncharted waters. Consider the stark contrast between a daydreamer and a missionary. Both might have grand visions, but it's the missionary who transforms those visions into tangible realities, bridging the gap between imagination and execution. A daydreamer remains tied to the shore of wishful thinking, content with "what ifs," while the missionary sets sail, navigating the currents of purpose and action. As the old saying highlights the futility of passive desire, **"If all wishes were horses, even the sluggard would ride."** The "horses"—the means to achieve goals—are reserved for those who possess the drive and determination to "go places." They understand that knowledge without action is useless, and vision without implementation is merely a mirage.

The missionary isn't just aware of what needs to be done; they feel compelled to do it. Driven by a purpose that transcends personal comfort, they are the architects of change. In contrast, the daydreamer, despite perhaps understanding what's needed, remains trapped by inaction, their potential unfulfilled, their impact negligible. The key difference lies in the gap between thinking and doing. The missionary, propelled by purpose, acts as a catalyst for change, embodying the principle that faith without works is dead. True impact comes not from idle thought, but from courageous action, stepping out in faith and pursuing vision with unwavering determination.

The Crucial Difference Between Knowing and Doing

Aristotle's profound observation, **"In practical matters the end is not mere speculative knowledge of what is to be done, but rather the doing of it,"** captures a timeless truth that applies to every human endeavor. He brilliantly highlights the crucial difference between knowing and doing. Knowledge, when isolated to mere theoretical contemplation, remains dormant, like a seed that never sprouts. It's only when knowledge is combined with action—when it's translated into tangible effort and applied to real-world situations—that it becomes a powerful force for transformation. The act of doing breathes life into knowledge, giving it purpose, direction, and impact. It's the difference between understanding how a car works and actually driving it. Aristotle's wisdom speaks to the essence of practical wisdom: the ability to effectively apply knowledge to achieve desired outcomes.

Consider the aspiring musician who carefully studies music theory but never practices an instrument, or the budding entrepreneur with a brilliant business plan who never launches their venture. In each case, knowledge remains stagnant, its potential unrealized. It is action—the courageous step forward, the persistent effort, the unwavering commitment to implementation—that unlocks the transformative power of knowledge. It is in the doing that we discover our capabilities, refine our skills, and achieve our goals. It is in the doing that we shape our realities and leave our mark on the world.

Seizing the Present Moment

> ***"How long will you wait before you begin to take possession of the land that the LORD, the God of your fathers, has given you?" (Joshua 18:3).***

This question, posed to the Israelites, resonates with a timeless urgency, a call to action that echoes through generations. It speaks to the danger of procrastination, the folly of waiting for perfect circumstances, and the necessity of seizing the present moment.

Self-preparation, while undeniably valuable, must be understood as a crucial stepping stone, not the final destination. It's the essential foundation for self-achievement, the launching pad from which you propel yourself towards your goals. Don't procrastinate. The time for action is now. Delaying what's inevitable or necessary only diminishes momentum and erodes confidence. Fear, that treacherous whisper of doubt, is a formidable adversary, but inaction—the refusal to confront fear and choose stagnation—is a far greater threat, a silent killer of dreams. By embracing action, by stepping out in faith, by confronting challenges head-on, you open the door to divine favor and the realization of your potential.

"You will never know until you try, you will never be until you go." This simple yet profound statement expresses the essence of progress. It highlights the importance of taking initiative, of stepping out in faith, and of venturing into the unknown. We discover what we're meant to do not by just thinking about it, but by actually doing something. It's about taking steps, big or small, to turn our visions and dreams into reality.

The Promise of Action

> ***"Every place that the sole of your foot shall tread upon, that have I given unto you" (Joshua 18:3).***

This promise, a declaration of divine provision, is contingent upon action. It is a reminder that opportunities are not passively received, but actively claimed. It is a call to explore, to venture forth, and to claim the territory that is rightfully ours.

> ***"It's better to begin and fail than to complain and laugh at those trying. Failing teaches you; complaining sears your mind. Even eagles learn to fly by trying. Try today."***

This concise statement captures a fundamental truth about growth. Failure, often seen as negative, is actually an invaluable source of learning, a practical classroom where lessons are deeply ingrained. Complaining, on the other hand, is a corrosive poison that stifles creativity and breeds stagnation. Embrace the spirit of the eagle, which learns to soar through trial and error, through the courageous act of taking flight, even if it means a temporary tumble.

> Theodore Roosevelt's powerful words also ring true: ***"Far better it is to dare mighty things, to win glorious triumphs, even though checkered by failure, than to take rank with those poor spirits who neither enjoy much nor suffer much, because they live in the gray twilight that knows not victory nor defeat."***

His sentiment speaks to the importance of living a life of purpose and passion. True fulfillment comes not from avoiding challenges, but from confronting them head-on. The fear of failure should never outweigh the desire to achieve your dreams.

"It is by trying that winning happens." This brief statement captures the essence of achievement. Success is not a matter of chance, but a result of deliberate effort, of persistent attempts, and of unwavering determination. It is through the act of trying, through the willingness to risk failure, that we unlock the potential for victory.

A Legacy of Impact

Dr. Myles Munroe's powerful observation that the cemetery is **"the richest place on earth"** delivers a sobering truth—a stark reminder of the tragedy of untapped potential. It speaks to the profound loss of lives lived with unused gifts, unrealized dreams, and unfulfilled purposes. To die with talents buried and potential dormant is to leave a legacy of regret, a testament to a life unlived. We aren't born merely to exist, but to flourish, to be stewards of our unique talents, to cultivate them diligently, and to share them generously, enriching the lives of others and fulfilling our God-given purpose.

"It matters not how long we live, but how." This timeless wisdom cuts through the illusion that longevity alone equates to a meaningful life. A life's measure isn't its duration, but its impact—the depth of its influence and the breadth of its contribution. Our lives should be a living testament to service, a beacon of hope, and a source of inspiration. We are called to be contributors, builders, sowers of seeds that will blossom into a harvest of goodness.

> Ultimately, ***"On the day of your birth, people asked what to give you to make your life better. On the day of your death, people should be able to look at your work and see how you have made their lives better."***

This perfectly expresses the essence of a life well-lived. We are born not to consume, but to contribute; not to take, but to give. Our legacy should be defined by the lives we've touched, the problems we've solved, and the world we've improved.

The message is clear: do not wait for the perfect moment, for it may never arrive. Do not allow fear or doubt to paralyze you. Instead, embrace the present moment, take the first step, and begin your journey. The land of opportunity awaits, and it is through your action, your determination, and your unwavering belief that you will claim your inheritance. Do not merely dream; act. Do not merely plan; execute. Do not merely hope; strive. It is in the arena of action that destinies are forged, and dreams are realized.

Factors Necessary to a Successful Entrepreneurial Pursuit (Resulting from Self-Preparation):

Courage:

The will to subdue fear.

Perseverance:

The will to keep trying.

Persistence:

The will to continue despite opposition.

Love:

The will to overcome selfishness in serving.

Courage:

Fear often paralyzes us, preventing us from taking even a single step toward our dreams. It's a silent destroyer, an invisible barrier that holds us captive in a realm of "what ifs" and "could haves." Courage, however, is the antidote—the liberating force that separates those who start from those who don't, the doers from the dreamers. It scorns the very root of fear, dismantling its power and freeing us from its grip. The world, yearning for progress and transformation, desperately needs courageous individuals willing to stand tall in the face of adversity and blaze a trail for others to follow. A single act of bravery can ignite a movement, inspiring others and making ordinary people extraordinary. Courage transforms individuals into catalysts for change, beacons of hope, and living examples of human potential.

Courage isn't the absence of fear or an ignorant belief that challenges don't exist. Rather, it's the mastery of fear—the ability to acknowledge it, confront it head-on, and still move forward. It means stepping outside your comfort zone, embracing upcoming challenges, and venturing into the unknown with unwavering determination. Courage is the catalyst that transforms potential into action, igniting the engine of progress.

Action truly separates those who succeed from those who don't. This captures a fundamental truth about achievement. In life's arena, and in pursuit of our goals, action—not mere intention—determines the outcome. Those who dare to act, take risks, embrace the unknown, and venture beyond the familiar are the ones who ultimately prevail, achieve their dreams, and leave their mark on the world.

It's crucial to understand that courage isn't a gift bestowed upon a select few; it's a choice—a decision to confront fear and embrace action. Recognize that fear is a natural human emotion, but it doesn't have to define you. The greatest rewards often lie on the other side of our greatest fears. Let's cultivate courage, embrace action, and refuse to be defined by fear. Let's be the courageous individuals the world so desperately needs, inspiring others to step out of their comfort zones and pursue their dreams with unwavering determination. By embracing the power of action and the transformative force of courage, we choose to be winners, not losers.

Life, with its complex blend of experiences, is rarely a smooth or predictable journey. It's a dynamic and often challenging endeavor, marked by both triumphs and trials. However, it's within these challenges that the seeds of opportunity are sown, waiting to be discovered by those with the courage to seek them. Courageous people, those who refuse to be defined by their circumstances, are the architects of their own destinies, creating opportunities where others see only limitations.

Don't let fear numb you, paralyze your potential, or extinguish the flame of your dreams. While fear is a natural human emotion—a primal instinct designed to protect us from perceived threats—when it dominates our lives, it transforms from a protective mechanism into a crippling constraint, preventing us from reaching our full potential. Instead, choose courage—the antidote to fear, the catalyst for action, and the key that unlocks the door to a life of purpose and fulfillment.

Life isn't a passive experience or a spectator sport. It's an active, participatory journey where we're called to engage, contribute, and create. Challenges are an inevitable part of the human experience, but they are not insurmountable barriers. Courage empowers us to overcome obstacles, transforming setbacks into stepping stones and building bridges across what others perceive as unbridgeable divides, ultimately creating opportunities where others see only limitations. Remember, courage isn't the absence of fear, but the ability to act in spite of it. Fear can serve as a signal, not a stop sign—an indication that we're venturing into uncharted territory, exploring the boundaries of our potential. Often, the biggest rewards come after we overcome our fears, as stepping through what challenges us can lead to the greatest gains.

Life is a challenge; nothing comes on a silver platter. You have to earn your way. Those who set the stage for others, creating opportunities and industries, are the ones courageous enough to venture beyond what others only dream of. You are perfectly capable of setting up the ladder for the world to climb, more than able to start something that will attract ambitious people. With courage, you are well able to set and raise a standard for others to live up to. The businesses and employment markets you see today didn't always exist. They were brought into being because someone was courageous enough to start something. In the same way, you can also start something today, because all entrepreneurs and business people are just like you.

Entrepreneurs aren't born with extraordinary abilities or inherent advantages; they are ordinary people who choose to embrace courage, step outside their comfort zones, and transform their visions into reality. Entrepreneurship isn't the exclusive domain of a privileged few or a realm reserved for those with inherited wealth or elite connections. It is a path open to anyone with the courage to pursue their vision, challenge the status quo, disrupt conventional thinking, and create something of value that addresses a real need in the world. Ideas are only valuable when put into action.

> As Peter F. Drucker wisely observed, ***"Markets are not created by God, nature or economic forces but by businessmen."***

This highlights the active role entrepreneurs play in shaping the economic landscape. Markets aren't static or predetermined by fate; they are dynamic ecosystems, constantly evolving and adapting, shaped by the actions of entrepreneurs who dare to innovate, create, and serve. It is through innovation—introducing new ideas, products, and services—through creativity—thinking outside the box to find novel solutions—and through a relentless pursuit of customer satisfaction—an unwavering commitment to meeting and exceeding needs—that markets are created and transformed. Entrepreneurs are the architects of market change, the catalysts for economic growth, and the drivers of societal progress. They aren't just business people; they are problem solvers, innovators, and risk-takers. They are the ones who see opportunities where others see obstacles, who dare to challenge conventional wisdom, and who are willing to take the leap of faith to bring their visions to life. Therefore, let's cultivate the courage to set standards, challenge the status quo, and start something meaningful. Let's embrace the entrepreneurial spirit, recognizing that we are all capable of creating value, driving change, and making a positive impact on the world.

What step will you take today to cultivate your own courage and embrace action?

Persistence and Perseverance:

One cannot think of great persons without thinking of persistence and perseverance.

This profound statement, coupled with the equally insightful advice, **"When the going gets tough and rough, change of direction should not mean change of focus,"** perfectly captures a fundamental truth about achieving anything significant. It highlights that true greatness isn't born from ease, but from the unwavering commitment to a goal, even when challenges force a change in approach. The journey to success, to realizing one's full potential, is rarely a smooth, uninterrupted ascent. It is more often a winding path, fraught with setbacks, detours, and unexpected obstacles that test our resolve and challenge our resilience. Persistence and perseverance, those twin pillars of unwavering determination, are the qualities that enable us to navigate these challenges, to stay the course when others would falter, and to ultimately reach our destination.

The road to success may be difficult, demanding sacrifice and unwavering commitment. You need persistence and perseverance to endure the inevitable trials, to weather the storms that threaten to derail your progress. Rest, when necessary, to replenish your strength and renew your spirit, but never, under any circumstances, quit. Encourage yourself, speak words of affirmation into your own heart, and remind yourself of the purpose that drives you. Your gift, your unique contribution to the world, is needed, now more than ever.

Setbacks are not roadblocks, insurmountable barriers that halt our progress. They are opportunities for growth, invaluable lessons disguised as disappointments. It is through resilience, the ability to bounce back from adversity, through unwavering determination, the refusal to surrender to doubt, and through an unwavering belief in our vision, the unshakeable conviction that our dreams are attainable, that we ultimately achieve our goals and realize our potential.

"It is because of God's love for others that you were allowed to be born." This profound truth highlights the purposeful nature of our existence, the divine intention behind our creation. We are not here by chance, a random occurrence in a vast and indifferent universe. We are here to serve, to contribute, and to make a positive impact on the world, to be instruments of God's love and agents of His grace.

Use your gift to create opportunities for others, to lift them up, to empower them to achieve their own dreams. Never quit on your purpose, never abandon your vision. If you see it, if you can envision it, you can achieve it, with God's help.

Our gifts are not meant to be hoarded, to be kept locked away, but to be shared generously with the world. By using our talents to create opportunities for others, to open doors that would otherwise remain closed, we not only fulfill our own potential, but we also empower others to do the same, creating a ripple effect of positive change that extends far beyond our own reach. We become catalysts for transformation, agents of hope, and living examples of the power of persistence and perseverance.

To achieve victory, you must run with perseverance, always remembering that no win comes without conquering. Choosing not to conquer is choosing not to be victorious. You can only expect to win the prize if you actually run the race. Spectators don't run; they aren't participants. They only live to tell stories, not to wear medals or crowns, because every prize has a price, and only those who pay it get the reward. You have everything it takes to run your race to destiny, because God watches over you and gives power to complete every good work to the one who begins.

Achievement, particularly in the realm of meaningful endeavors, is not a passive experience, but an active pursuit. It demands unwavering dedication, relentless effort, and the willingness to endure hardship. The journey towards victory requires conquering not only external obstacles, but also the internal battles against doubt, fear, and complacency.

Success, in its truest form, demands sacrifice. It requires a willingness to endure hardship, overcome seemingly insurmountable obstacles, and fully invest the time, energy, and resources needed to bring our visions to life. It's about understanding that there are no shortcuts to lasting achievement; true success is earned through hard work, dedication, and unwavering commitment.

This truth is powerfully captured by the acronym C.R.O.W.N.: "Every reward has a COST known as a RISK for the reward. OVERCOMERS are those who pay the risk in order to WIN. And the right time for you to pay the cost, take the risk, overcome and win is NOW." This statement perfectly highlights that victory isn't free; it requires courageous action and an immediate commitment to facing challenges head-on.

> ***"If we shrink from the hard contests where men must win at the hazard of their lives and at the risk of all they hold dear, then bolder and stronger peoples will pass us by and will win for themselves the domination of the world." - Theodore Roosevelt.***

Roosevelt's words are a clarion call to action, a stark reminder that the world belongs to those who dare to compete, to take risks, and to strive for excellence. He challenges us to confront our fears, to embrace the challenges that lie before us, and to push ourselves beyond our perceived limitations.

Roosevelt's sentiment speaks to the importance of courage, resilience, and a competitive spirit. It's about recognizing that the world is not a passive stage, but an active arena where individuals and nations compete for influence and achievement. It's about understanding that those who are willing to embrace the challenges, to take the risks, and to persevere through adversity are the ones who ultimately shape the course of history.

It's about understanding that victory often requires pushing beyond comfort zones, and that there are prices to pay for the achievements we seek. It's about being willing to invest the effort, time, and sacrifice required to achieve our goals. It's about recognizing that the path to success is not always easy, but it is always worth it.

"You are more than a conqueror. Stay on course. Be persistent." This powerful declaration affirms our inherent capacity for triumph, our ability to rise above adversity and achieve victory in the face of challenges. It's a reminder that we are not passive victims of circumstance, but active agents of change, endowed with the strength and resilience to overcome any obstacle that stands in our path.

We are not defined by our circumstances, by the limitations that others may impose upon us, or by the setbacks we may encounter along the way. We are defined by our response to those circumstances, by our ability to choose resilience over resignation, determination over despair. We are capable of achieving any goal, realizing any dream, if we possess the unwavering will to persevere, to stay the course, and to refuse to surrender to doubt or discouragement.

This is not a call to blind optimism, but a recognition of our inherent potential, our God-given capacity to triumph over adversity. It's about cultivating a mindset of unwavering determination, a spirit that refuses to be defeated, a belief that anything is possible with persistence. It's about understanding that our true strength is not measured by the absence of challenges, but by our ability to overcome them.

Think of it like a marathon runner. The race is long and strenuous, filled with moments of exhaustion and doubt. But the runner who stays on course, who pushes through the pain, who refuses to give up, is the one who ultimately crosses the finish line. Similarly, in the marathon of life, it is those who persevere, who remain steadfast in their pursuit of their goals, who ultimately achieve victory.

Therefore, let us embrace our identity as more than conquerors, let us stay on course, unwavering in our commitment to our dreams, and let us cultivate the persistence that will enable us to overcome any obstacle and achieve our full potential. Let us choose to be defined not by our circumstances, but by our unwavering determination to triumph.

The Power of Love:

Love, in its purest form, acts as a unifying force, gently guiding every aspect of our lives toward a greater purpose. It's the invisible thread weaving together our relationships, sparking acts of kindness, and fueling the creation of lasting beauty. In stark contrast, selfish ambition, driven by the ego's endless hunger for personal gain, ultimately leads to emptiness. It's a hollow shell of self-importance that eventually crumbles under its own weight.

Unlike the temporary pleasures of selfish ambition, love is eternal. It leaves a lasting legacy of compassion and positive change, creating a ripple effect of goodness that reaches far beyond our own lives. Love is the bedrock upon which strong relationships are built, the driving force behind selfless service, and the true source of deep satisfaction.

Consider the difference between art made for personal fame and art created from a genuine love for beauty and expression. The first might receive temporary applause, but the latter resonates with timeless appeal, touching hearts and inspiring souls across generations. Love is the artist's hand, the musician's soul, the writer's heart, breathing a unique life force into their creations.

Selfish ambition, on the other hand, is a solitary pursuit—a lonely journey toward a destination that turns out to be an illusion. It builds walls between people, breeds resentment, and leaves a trail of broken connections. Love, conversely, builds bridges, fosters unity, and strengthens the bonds that connect us all. It's the glue that holds communities together, the force that drives positive social change, and the light that illuminates the path toward a more fair and compassionate world.

Love is more than just an emotion; it's a principle, a way of being, a force that shapes our character and defines our legacy. True success isn't measured by what we accumulate, but by what we give—by the love we share and the lives we touch. It's about living a life that is not just long, but loving, impactful, and eternally significant.

As the saying goes, **"Love is your mighty touch that turns everything you touch into gold."** This speaks to love's transformative power, its ability to elevate the ordinary to the magnificent, the commonplace to the extraordinary. This isn't about literal gold, of course, but about the immeasurable value love adds to our lives and the lives of those around us.

Love transforms routine actions into extraordinary acts of kindness and generosity. It infuses our work with purpose and meaning, elevating it beyond mere labor to a manifestation of our deepest values and most heartfelt intentions. It's the secret ingredient that turns a simple meal into a feast of fellowship, a daily task into an act of service, and a temporary moment into a lasting memory.

Imagine a gardener tending to their plants with love. Their touch is gentle, their care is precise, and their attention is unwavering. The result is not just a flourishing garden, but a vibrant design of life, a testament to love's transformative power. The same principle applies to every aspect of our lives. When we approach our work, our relationships, and our endeavors with love, we infuse them with a quality that transcends the ordinary—a golden touch that brings forth beauty, abundance, and joy.

Love is the catalyst that ignites creativity, fuels passion, and inspires selfless service. It's the force that heals wounds, mends broken hearts, and builds bridges between people. As expressed in 1 Corinthians 16:14, **"Let all things be done with love."** This is not merely a suggestion, but a fundamental principle for living a fulfilling life. Love should permeate every aspect of our existence, guiding our interactions, shaping our decisions, and defining our purpose.

> Furthermore, 1 Corinthians 13:13 reminds us, ***"And now these three remain: faith, hope and love. But the greatest of these is love."***

Faith and hope are essential pillars of a meaningful life, but love is the cornerstone upon which they rest. Love is the ultimate expression of our humanity, the force that binds us together, and the catalyst for positive change.

Finally, **"Love never fails,"** as stated in 1 Corinthians 13:8. Love is an enduring force, capable of overcoming any obstacle, healing any wound, and bridging any divide. Its impact extends beyond the temporal, creating a ripple effect that touches countless lives across generations. Love truly transcends failure, offering hope and renewal even in the face of despair.

In conclusion, the pursuit of vision is not a solitary endeavor, but a collective journey. It requires courage to confront our fears, perseverance to overcome obstacles, and persistence to stay the course. Most importantly, it demands a heart filled with love—a driving force that transforms our actions into acts of service and our lives into a legacy of compassion. Let us embrace the call to action, to pursue our visions with unwavering determination, and to leave the world a better place than we found it. Let our lives be a testament to the transformative power of love, a beacon of hope for generations to come.

11

Conclusion

As we draw this journey to a close, let us reflect on the ultimate purpose of our endeavors. Beyond the accumulation of material wealth and the attainment of worldly success, there lies a profound truth: at the end of all things, we will stand before God, called to account for the stewardship of our God-given gifts. It is not the mere possession of these gifts that matters, but the fruit they bear, the transformative impact they have on the world.

God's interest goes beyond the return of our talents in their original, untouched state. He yearns to witness the flourishing of these gifts, the tangible manifestation of their potential. The gift within you is a seed, a powerful grain of possibility, destined to be sown, cultivated, and harvested. It is through this process of active engagement, of diligent labor, that we produce the fruit that glorifies God and blesses humanity.

Fruitfulness, in its essence, is the very purpose of our creation. It is the lifeblood of our existence, the sustenance that nourishes both ourselves and those around us. When we embrace fruitfulness, we align ourselves with the divine design, becoming conduits of God's grace and provision. Conversely, a life devoid of fruitfulness, a life marked by inactivity and inaction, creates a perception of divine neglect. It is a state of profound spiritual danger, a transgression against the very purpose of our being. Unfruitfulness, like a barren fig tree or a buried talent, can attract a spiritual curse, a consequence of neglecting the divine mandate to create and contribute. (Refer to Matthew 21:19 and Matthew 25:24-26).

You were carefully crafted for a life of abundant fruitfulness. The present moment, while the breath of life sustains you, is the opportune time to cultivate and manifest your gifts. To depart from this world with your potential unrealized is similar to never having existed at all. The true chronicle of your life is not a birth certificate, but the indelible mark of your work on earth. Your existence extends beyond the physical realm, and it ceases not at the moment of death, but at the moment you choose to abandon your capacity to improve society.

Therefore, embrace the purpose that ordained your birth and existence. With unwavering focus and unwavering dedication, commit yourself to its fulfillment. Let no thought, no obstacle, deter you from living a productive life, a life brimming with creativity and innovation. Let courage be your steadfast companion, propelling you to initiate your endeavors. Let perseverance be your unwavering strength, sustaining you through trials and tribulations. Let persistence be your relentless drive, carrying you forward despite opposition. You are a missionary, a vessel of purpose, destined to accomplish and fulfill a divine mandate.

Let your workmanship illuminate the world, transforming it into a haven of progress and prosperity. When your earthly journey concludes, may you echo the words of the apostle Paul, declaring to your generation: "I have fought the good fight, I have finished the race, I have kept the faith. Now there is in store for me the crown of righteousness." (2 Timothy 4:7-8).

May the remainder of your life be the pinnacle of your existence, a testament to your unwavering commitment to your calling. You are a victor, an overcomer, and wealth, in its truest sense, is your rightful inheritance.

Made in the USA
Coppell, TX
08 June 2026

79224880R00121